Woodworking for the Serious Beginner

WOODWORKING FOR THE SERIOUS BEGINNER

Pamela Philpott-Jones & Paul L. McClure

Photos by Pamela Philpott-Jones
Drawings by Daniel R. Bishop

CAMBIUM PRESS

Dedications

PAUL: To my mother, Eula, and father, LaVern, who instilled in me a sense that I could accomplish anything I put my mind to, and encouraged me to pursue my interests.

To my brother, Ross, who took everything apart so I could learn how to fix it. And to my son, Sean, and his wife, Debbie—I could not wish for better children.

PAM: This book is loving dedicated to my mother, Victoria. Thanks for your help, I couldn't have done it without you.

CAMbIUM PRESS

First printing: October 1995
Printed in the United States of America

Cambium Press
PO Box 909
Bethel, CT 06801

Distributed to the trade by:
Lyons & Burford
31 w 21st St.
New York NY 10010
tel 212-620-9580   fax 212-929-1836

Library of Congress Cataloging in Publication Data

ISBN 0-9643999-2-X

Table of Contents

PAUL'S ACKNOWLEDGMENTS

The art of woodworking has traditionally been taught through a master/apprentice relationship. Those days are pretty much gone now, but I was fortunate over the past 35 years to have worked in the cabinetmaking trade and as a wood technologist with tradesmen and experts who answered my questions with unfailing patience. In so doing, they provided me with the in-depth knowledge and understanding that I am now able to impart to my students and to all those who are interested in woodworking. I am grateful to them all.

To Pam, my most fervent thanks. Without her, there would have been no book. The long hours and dedication that she put in deserve the highest accolades. Her never-ending questions, asked on behalf of beginners everywhere, made sure that this book became a truly useful source of practical information.

Special thanks are due to those colleagues who have freely given of their knowledge: Howard Sala, who encouraged me in high school to pursue a career in wood technology and woodworking; Tony Jacobs, for allowing me to sweep his shop and learn woodworking from a master; Frank Paxton, Jr., who imparted to me the ethics of doing business in the wood industry; Dr. Rod Anderson, who was instrumental in helping me develop a wood technology curriculum at Colorado State University; and Regis Miller, of the Forest Products Laboratory, who assisted me with wood technology.

Since this book is all about wood and tools, I must thank some of the people and manufacturers who have made it easier to produce high-quality woodworking: Bill Biesemeyer and Roger Thompson of Biesemeyer Manufacturing; Jim Mollenkopf and Eagle America; John Economaki of Bridge City Tool Works; Rich Johnson of the Woodworkers Store; Ray Rocchio of Paxton Beautiful Woods; Steve Cowles of Oak Lumber; and Jodi Davenport, of Woods, Inc. I would also like to thank Jeff Dodd, of the Craig Lumber Corp., for his sincere friendship and assistance in the international world of wood. Tom Pierce, a cabinetmaker of unparalled excellence, kindly provided unlimited access to his tools for photo purposes.

Thanks are also due to the individuals who had faith in my

writing and encouraged me to write for their publications: Larry Clayton, editor, and Peter J. Stephano, senior editor, of Better Homes and Gardens' WOOD magazine; and David Sloan, editor and publisher, Ellis Wallentine, executive editor, and Paul Anthony, assistant editor, of AMERICAN WOODWORKER magazine. Special thanks go to Rick Mastelli and Deborah Fillion, for their invaluable input into the first chapters of this book.

Thanks to my close friends and fellow woodworkers, Andy Trotti, Bill Lovelace, Ed Sargent, Morey Patten, Jack Ettinger, Joe Nagy, Dave Rieder, and Marlin McKenna for their in-depth questions pertaining to woodworking—they have greatly expanded my knowledge.

Lastly, my devoted thanks to my friend and long-time colleague in woodworking, Jim 'Ole Buzzard' Woodruff, who thinks he taught me everything I know, but if the truth be known, I learned it by teaching him and correcting his mistakes as well as my own.

PAM'S ACKNOWLEDGMENTS

For all their help in putting together this book, I wish to thank the following people:

Rick Mastelli, for his initial support and encouragement.

John Kelsey of Cambium Press, for realizing that woodworking novices needed—and deserved—a book of their own.

Laura Tringali, for her enthusiasm, guidance, and humor during the editing phase.

And the rest of the folks at Cambium: Daniel R. Rishop for his fine illustrations, scanner operator Morgan Kelsey, and Anita Pandolfi for her solid design work.

INTRODUCTION

PAM: I started dabbling in woodworking when I began restoring my house. I had watched all the "how-to" programs on TV and read the occasional "do-it-yourself" article in a magazine. How difficult could woodworking be, anyway? Before long, I had painted, or rather milled, myself into a corner. Frustrated as I was, I wouldn't give up—my financial investment in a combination machine, not to mention the lumber, was just too great.

Soon I decided my only recourse was to learn the fundamentals of woodworking. Unfortunately, this almost proved impossible. Although there was a college in my area that taught adult woodworking classes, the hours were inconvenient and the tuition was outrageous. I shifted into Plan B: Since I can read and follow instructions, I hit the book stores for the basic information I needed. Again, a dead end. The available literature, which was often pretty intimidating, seemed to assume that I already knew at least something about woodworking. I began to panic. Just where was a beginner supposed to go for help?

As a last resort, I started attending woodworking seminars at a local hardwoods lumberyard, and there I met Paul McClure. He was lecturing on wood technology, an interesting subject, but of no use to the beginner—who cares about all the different woods if you can't do anything with them? After the seminar, I explained my dilemma to Paul. He was sympathetic; over the years he had taught woodworking and helped many a beginner get started on the path to building fine furniture.

This book arose from my experiences with woodworking in Paul's shop. As a writer, the big advantage I had over other authors was that I really was a beginner. Alone in the shop with Paul I could ask—and record—the elementary questions that in a seminar might cause more experienced woodworkers to snicker.

In writing this book, Paul and I assumed that its readers would know nothing about woodworking, but would be eager to learn.

New old way of measuring

We also decided to teach readers how to use the time-honored, accurate method of building furniture with story poles and transfer of measurement rather than with tape measures. I've bungled more wood by measuring it with a tape than anything else. Most books give you specific measurements for the pieces you are to build, and it certainly is much easier on the author and editors than trying to explain how to transfer measurements. However, attempting to re-configure a pre-measured piece can be a nightmare. By contrast, once you understand how to transfer measurements, you can customize any design to suit your needs. Realizing that some people might not initially feel comfortable with all this freedom, at the beginning of each project we have included the measurements that I used to build my shop furniture. Use those figures if you must, but keep in mind that they might not accommodate your needs.

A step-by-step process

This is a step-by-step book: You learn certain building procedures in the first project that are carried over into the next project. Furthermore, we don't throw a whole bunch of new techniques at you in each project; instead, we enhance the techniques you are already learning. If you skip a project, you will miss a lot. So even if you already have a workbench, please don't skip building the one we have included here. Build a small one if you like and call it a sharpening bench, but you need to get the experience of measuring, milling, and building each project before you continue to the next.

Acquiring your machines and tools is also a step-by-step process. You needn't run right out and purchase everything just to get started—neither the extension table nor the workbench require a router, for example. Each project has a tool list; refer to it to see what you have and what you need to buy.

Finally, as a beginner, expect to make mistakes. Let me dispel a typical myth that woodworking is easy—it's not. Woodworking is a craft, and, as with any other craft it takes time and plenty of practice and patience, to learn. Yet the fun you will have in the process is well worth the investment. Enough said—let's get started.

1 WHAT TO BUY

The Table Saw

PAM: Why do you need a table saw? Good question. There are plenty of other saws available; in the power-tool department there are the portable circular saw, jigsaw, trim saw, power miter box, and chain saw. If worse comes to worse, there are always hand saws, just in case you're miles from any electrical outlets. All these saws are less expensive and certainly don't take up as much room as a table saw. Plus, you can haul them around, taking the saw to the job instead of the job to the saw.

So why bother with a table saw? A table saw will do everything that all the portable power saws mentioned above can do and more—it can rip, crosscut, and cut angles (including compound angles), as well as cut dadoes, rabbets, and numerous other joints, all accurately. And "accurately" is the key word here, because accurately milled parts that produce tight-fitting joints are the most important elements of a finely crafted piece of furniture.

Oh sure, a table saw looks big and intimidating compared to the portable power saws, but when used correctly, you, as the operator, have control over every aspect of the milling process. First off, you're not freehanding a cut with a running blade that may or may not have a guard between you and the blade. Trip over a cord, lose control of the stock being cut, or worse, the tool cutting the stock, and you're in big trouble. By contrast, as the operator of a table saw, you usually have wood between your hand and the machine. If your hand slips across the top of the wood being cut, you will cut yourself, but chances are you won't cut anything off. Furthermore, as the operator, you have control over the guards, hold-downs, pushsticks, and pushblocks that prevent your hands from coming near the running blade. While it's sometimes easier to break down large stock or sheets of particleboard or plywood with a circular saw or jigsaw, you'll always have to remill the wood accurately with the table saw. If you build the extension tables shown in Chapter 6, you'll find you can easily saw large sheet materials as well as long and/or wide boards with your table saw. The bottom line: If you are serious about woodworking, you need a table saw.

PAUL: A table saw is the workhorse of the shop, and the biggest investment you will make. There are so many saws on the market that deciding what is right for you can make your head swim. I suggest you take the time to do a bit of research. After you've narrowed down the choices, buy the best saw you can afford, because you will likely have this tool for life.

A table saw seems like a huge investment, but it's the one tool you can't do without. All table saws have a slot where the blade comes through, a long fence (right) for ripping, an elevation mechanism and a tilt mechanism.

What type of table saw should you buy? We'll look at the basic options: the bench saw (cheap), the contractor's saw (more expensive), and the cabinet saw (most expensive). Other than cost, there are three things to consider when purchasing a table saw: power, the fence, and the safety guard. Power is a function of the motor and drive system, which is what determines a superior saw.

The motor and drive system

PAUL: Let's look at the motor first. When buying a saw, you need to look at the amperage, or amps. Forget horsepower—it's a vague term. A manufacturer might rate the horsepower of its motor at continuous load or peak load (the point just before the motor burns out). And since the manufacturer won't tell you what load measurement was used to determine the horsepower, you have no way of knowing what horsepower the motor actually delivers. A better way to determine how much power a motor can deliver is by amperage. Current (amperage, or amps) is a ratio of V/R (V = voltage, R = resistance) in the motor. Amperage is determined by the motor manufacturer and cannot be altered. The higher the amperage, the more power the motor will deliver. And in this situation, the more amperage, the better. On a table saw, 13 amps is the lowest you should go.

After the motor, the next thing to consider is the drive system that moves the blade—direct drive or pulley/belt. The issue here is how much power is actually delivered to the sawblade from the motor. Typically, the normal vibrations of a saw in use cause a considerable amount of loss between the power that the motor is putting out and the power that the arbor (the threaded steel shaft the sawblade is mounted on) is receiving. If there is too much power loss, the overworked motor may quit in the middle of a cut. This can happen when trying to saw hardwoods, but if the motor is really

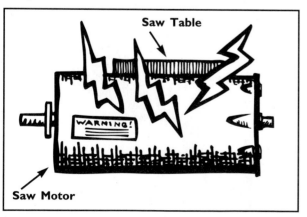

On a direct-drive saw, the blade mounts directly onto the motor shaft. The motor's bulk mans the blade can't be raised for a deep cut.

underpowered, it won't even be able to cut soft-woods. Usually, the first reaction of the operator is to back the board out of the blade; once free, the blade starts turning again, possibly kicking the board out of the saw and back toward the operator (a phenomenon called kickback)—a nasty surprise.

There are three different arrangements that try to overcome the power-loss predicament: the direct-drive system, the single pulley/belt system, and the triple pulley/belt system.

Direct-drive system—Here the motor shaft is also the arbor. Although this sequence transfers 100 percent of the power from the motor to the blade, there is one major disadvantage. A pulley-and-belt system (even when there are three assemblies, as with a cabinet saw) can be overpowered by jammed or warped boards, which will stop the blade. By contrast, if you

The mechanism inside a contractor-style table saw allows the blade to raise and tilt while the motor stays put.

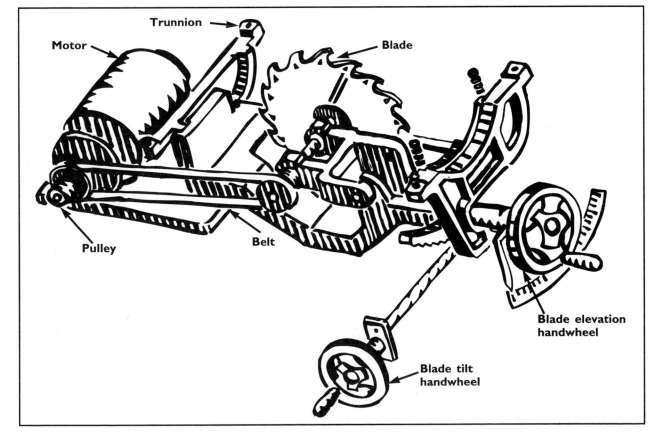

Multiple belts drive professional-grade saws.

bind the blade on a direct-drive saw, the motor still keeps trying to turn, and since the motor can't turn the arbor, the windings heat up and the wires burn through—causing motor burnout. And if you burnout the motor, you have to replace it, which can cost more than the saw did in the first place.

Single pulley/belt system—The single pulley/belt system is driven by a motor mounted on a hinge at the back of the saw. The hinge allows the motor to adjust as the blade is raised and lowered. A hinged motor has a tendency to bounce, and bounce equals vibration, so the belt will start to slip as it periodically loses contact with the pulley that is driving it. This may be perceived as a disadvantage, because the belt doesn't transfer 100 percent of the power from the motor to the blade. However, the belt slippage adds a certain margin of safety: The blade will stop if a board is jammed, allowing time to shut off the saw, and, ultimately, saving the motor from burning out. Pulley/belt systems will not prevent kickback, but they are safer because of the pulley/belt arrangement.

Triple pulley/belt system—This system solves the problem of power transfer. The motor is bolted in tandem with the arbor and moves as one unit when the blade is raised or tilted, thereby allowing the three belts to be permanently tightened, reducing slippage and transferring 99 percent of the power to the blade. This design produces tremendous power and can handle just about any cutting situation a woodworker might require. Yet if a board does get jammed, and it doesn't often happen with these powerful saws, the blade will stop, giving you time to shut off the saw.

Types of saws

PAUL: With all this in mind, let's take a look at the different table saws.

Bench saw—This is the least desirable saw to purchase. It has two disadvantages: First, it has a direct-drive system; second, its smallness and portability (it doesn't come with legs) make it much less solid than other types of saws. And the miter gauge is a joke. (The miter gauge consists of a little fence attached to a bar that travels in a slot machined in the table-saw surface parallel to the sawblade.) Usually, a protractor scale is etched into the fence; by loosening the handle, the fence can pivot right or left to obtain any desired angle. There are positive stops for the most common angles built into the fence/protractor assembly. The miter gauge that comes with a bench saw is tiny and much too small to support anything but tiny stock. Also, a bench saw simply doesn't have the power to cut dense hardwoods such as maple, cherry, oak, and walnut.

The motor hangs off the back of most contractor-style table saws. You can buy a new contractor's saw for $350-$700, depending on quality and accessories.

So I bought a contractor's saw....

PAM: *I absolutely needed a saw. The combination machine I had bought was a sorry excuse for a table saw (Chapter 2), and I was tired of living with the limitations it imposed. Paul waxed poetic for days about a cabinet saw—everything was junk compared to this saw. Paul's idea was that since I was graduating from one saw to another, and I was committed to woodworking, I should get the best. He had me convinced that I had to have a cabinet saw, until I found out how much it would cost. Big bucks! At this point in my career I knew quite a few woodworkers, so I asked around: Who was using what? And I found out that unless the person was a professional woodworker, or had come by his or her cabinet saw secondhand, the contractor's saw was by far the most popular choice. So I bought a contractor's saw, by mail order.*

If you purchase your saw this way, there are a few things you should know. My 250-lb. saw arrived in pieces, and was dropped off at my back door. It was no small feat for Paul and me to carry the parts down to my basement shop. When we got to the cast-iron table, we had to use a dolly. So be prepared, and have someone there to help you. Also, assembling the saw required wrenches: A set of socket wrenches came in handy. The directions were fairly straightforward, yet it took time to assemble, as everything had to be aligned. Putting together your own saw has its advantages—you really get to know the machine, up close and personal. We did have problems with the fence, and the guard was almost impossible to install. I'll tell you about that in the guard and fence sections.

The substantial enclosed base of a cabinet saw houses the motor, multiple-pulley drive, and electrical system. This saw has an overarm guard.

Contractor's saw—Although a contractor's saw is larger than a bench saw, it's still portable, made to be moved (by at least two strong bodies) from one job site to another. Pam uses a contractor's saw—it weighs around 250 lbs., and needless to say, she doesn't move it around very much.

Contractor's saws are preferred by most beginners since they are larger and safer than bench saws, but don't cost as much as cabinet saws. They come with a single pulley/belt drive system, and are solid enough to handle large stock. There are many different contractor's saws to choose from, and while all of them take up about the same amount of shop space, how much power the different motors can deliver varies. You want to look for a powerful motor (at least 13 amps, approximately $1^1/2$ horsepower), and enough weight (225 to 300 lbs.) to lend stability and reduce vibration. Beware of lightweight contractor's saws, which are really just direct-drive bench saws with legs.

Cabinet saw—These large, stable machines produce tremendous power, and are favored by professionals and experienced cabinetmakers. They have a triple pulley/belt drive system with the motor (and drive system) encased in a metal cabinet beneath the table; the weight adds stability when handling large stock and helps minimize vibration. With a contractor's saw, the belt (only one) can't be adjusted for tension because the hinged motor has to independently moved in or out as the blade is raised, lowered, or tilted at an angle. It's the motor's weight that causes the tension between the pulley and belt. However, with a cabinet saw, the motor/arbor/pulley system is built as one carriage; when the blade is raised, lowered, or tilted, the carriage moves as one unit on the trunnions (carriage supports). This arrangement allows for all three belts to be adjusted

Look for a saw table made of cast iron, not sheet steel or aluminum. This model has stamped metal table extensions, which are good, and a standard Delta-type rip fence.

for transferring maximum power from the motor to the arbor.

I have owned a cabinet saw for years, and would recommend one to anybody. However, this isn't a saw usually purchased by beginners because of the expense. Instead, get yourself a good, heavy, medium-priced contractor's saw; it will last a lifetime and should handle all of your projects. If at a later date you become completely committed to woodworking and want the best, a cabinet saw is the way to go.

Saw tables and arbors

PAUL: The table on a good-quality saw is flat and smooth. It is flat so that it won't distort any given cut, and smooth so it won't damage the lumber. Cast iron is preferred over steel because it adds weight, won't warp, and can be machined to high tolerances. All cabinet saws have cast-iron tops, as do most contractor's saws. However, contractor's saws have table

The fence on the table saw must permit side-to-side adjustment.

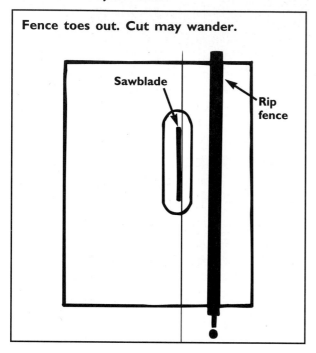

Fence toes out. Cut may wander.

Sawblade

Rip fence

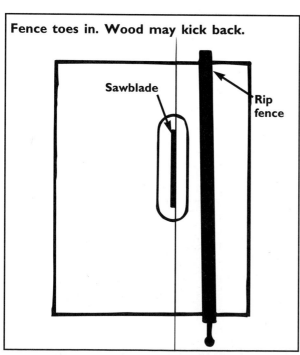

Fence toes in. Wood may kick back.

Sawblade

Rip fence

extensions on either side of the cast iron to enlarge the table to a usable size (equivalent to that of a cabinet saw). These extensions are either webbed cast iron or stamped steel; steel is used to make the saw less expensive and lighter in weight, so it can be moved around construction sites. The problem with a webbed top is that your fingers can get stuck in it, or the wood, or both, but you can get used to working with one. On the other hand, stamped steel extensions might warp. It's your choice.

Avoid aluminum tables at all costs. Aluminum will oxidize, forming a fine gray powder that will discolor light-colored woods, such as maple, resulting in the need for additional sanding and finishing work. And since aluminum is soft, it scratches easily. If you have an aluminum top, protect it with a coating of high-quality wax.

Whatever type of table saw you buy, make sure it has a tilting arbor (meaning that the blade tilts) rather than a tilting table. Tilting tables are available primarily on combination machines, discussed in the next chapter; they're just too inaccurate for high-quality work.

The fence

PAUL: The fence on any tool is used to guide the work through the cut, but its main function is to support the wood, preventing it from being pulled from your grip by the sawblade. On a table saw, the fence is a long metal guide that spans the table from front to back. It should be parallel to the blade, and herein lies the problem—most of the fences that come with table saws are difficult to keep aligned with the blade because they simultaneously lock down on the front and the back rails. As the fence clamp-hooks wear on the front and back rails, the back of the fence will either toe in or toe out. If the back of the fence toes in, the rear part of the fence will be closer to the blade than the front part. Since the back of the sawblade is turning up, the board can be picked up off the table and thrown back toward the operator. If the back of the fence toes out, the rear part of the fence is farther away from the blade than the front part of the fence. Therefore, a board being ripped is against the fence when the cut is started, but not against the fence as the board clears the blade. At this point, the fence no longer supports the board, making the board difficult to control—and if you loose control of the board, you risk serious injury. While most fences that come with contractor's saws will perform properly if they are constantly maintained, the fences on most bench saws are unusable, even dangerous. These fences are too short (because the table is small), don't lock down accurately, and are hard to adjust to parallel. In some instances, the fence won't lock down tightly and will come loose during the cut—very dangerous.

Your cut is only as good as your fence, so when buying a saw, consider the following: How easy is it to adjust the fence? Are there increments that line up? Are the markings easy

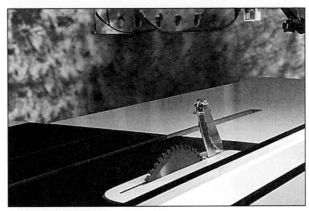

This saw has a splitter with anti-kickback pawls. The splitter keeps the cut wood from pinching the blade.

to read? Can the fence accommodate jigs and fixtures? Does it stay in place once it's locked down? If the fence can be adjusted easily, but moves even slightly when you lock it down, you won't get an accurate cut.

I chose to replace the fence that came with my saw with an after-market fence (see photo). "After-market" means that an independent manufacturer makes an accessory intended for

If the sawblade grabs the wood, the pawls dig into the surface and keep it from kicking back.

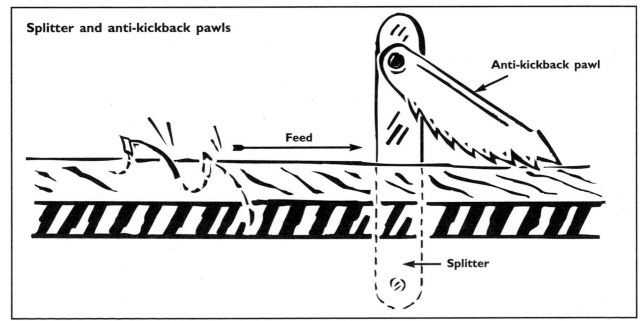

Splitter and anti-kickback pawls

Anti-kickback pawl

Feed

Splitter

use with a certain tool. An after-market fence operates more accurately, is easier to use, and usually eliminates the problem of toeing in and out. The one I bought comes with its own rail, which replaces the front rail on the table saw. It has a better measuring system; instead of the crudely stamped measuring increments and inaccurate metal pointer, an after-market fence is outfitted with a tape, similar to a tape measure, that rests on top of the rail. The front of the fence is fitted with a plastic window with a hairline marker to read the tape measure. The marker can be adjusted to exactly zero when the fence is against the blade, and from then on, the fence can be set precisely to width. Even if you look at the hairline marker from any other angle than straight on, you will still get an accurate reading. The fence can be adjusted right or left of the blade, depending on whether you are right- or left-handed. Since most after-market fences only lock down on the front rail, the toe-in, toe-out problem is virtually eliminated; the fence is easily squared to exactly 90 degrees to the front rail and parallel to the blade, and easily readjusted, if needed, with very little time expended. An after-market fence will move effortlessly across the table, making the fence easy to position; you don't have to mess around tapping the fence into place. And because of the simple design, various jigs and fixtures can be easily adapted to an after-market fence.

PAM: Here again, Paul was leading me down the path of the most expensive. Did I really need an after-market fence? The fence I had been using on my combination machine (next chapter) was a disaster. It could not, would not, lock down in place. Whenever I locked it, it moved a faction of an inch to either side. Trying to compensate for the movement drove me crazy. So when I bought my contractor's saw and started using the fence that came with it, I was pleased. A person can only

appreciate a superior fence if an inferior one has been used. However, after about a year of working with my fence, I began to experience some of the problems that Paul describes. The main problem was that the fence wouldn't always lock down accurately—the same problem I had with the fence on my combination machine. Yes, out there on the horizon, I can see that after-market fence looming.

The saw guard

PAUL: A saw guard is supposed to keep your fingers away from the blade—an important goal. But the guard that typically comes with a bench or contractor's saw leaves something to be desired. Most guards have a thin sheet of metal that attaches the guard to the saw and acts as a splitter, keeping the cut (kerf) from closing after exiting the blade. Yet the kerf usually closes farther down the cut, well after it has cleared the splitter. A board that is pinching the blade can also require more force to push through the cut, which is a safety hazard.

The major drawback to a standard guard with a splitter is that it will not allow you to cut grooves or dadoes. The guard has to be removed, since the splitter will block the board from passing through the blade. After having to remove the guard a few times for different cuts, I took the guard off and replaced it with an after-market guard and splitter. The saw guard is attached by a long arm to the right or left edge of the table saw. It covers a much larger area than the thin guards that come with most saws, and you can leave an after-market guard in place for dadoing, rabbeting, and angle cuts. However, using just the after-market guard will not prevent kickback, so you really need an after-market splitter with pawls, such as the one shown in the drawing. Buy a splitter that can be attached (in the location of the original splitter,) and that can be quickly engaged and disengaged.

After-market fences, guards, and splitters can be purchased through woodworking mail-order catalogs, large specialty woodworking dealers, and woodworking shows. Yes, it costs more money to get an after-market guard system, but there is no price too high for safety. **PAM:** I have had more problems with saw guards than anything else in my shop. I'm a beginner, and a beginner is supposed to use a guard—period. Yet everyone I knew worked without a guard. And after spending an entire afternoon trying to get the guard aligned with the blade on my combination machine, I started understanding why. AN IMPORPERLY ALIGNED SAW GUARD IS MORE DANGEROUS THAN NOT HAVING ONE AT ALL! I cannot stress this enough. I had more kickback from my guard than anything else. Since the guard was not perfectly aligned over the sawblade, the splitter was pinching the wood against the fence after it had cleared the blade, and this was causing kickback. I also had to force my wood through the cut since it was binding in the splitter. Of course, no one tells you about these things until it is too late. After spending hours working on the guard, I was finally able to shim the darn thing and got it to work. But every time I removed the guard to cut dadoes or reconfigure the machine, I had to realign and shim the guard when I put it back on. Needless to say, this took up a fair amount of time, and the whole process became a regular nightmare.

When I bought my contractor's saw, I was thrilled at the thought of having a guard that worked. Unfortunately, this wasn't the case. The guard on my table saw proved to be even more temperamental than the one on my combination machine. I couldn't install it. Paul couldn't install it. Paul kept insisting that we didn't use it at all, but I wouldn't relent. I wanted that guard in place and working properly. After hours of complaining, Paul finally figured

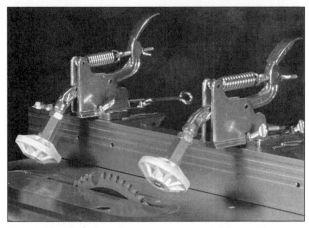

Anti-kickback wheels mounted on the rip fence help feed the wood safely. If the saw kicks back, the wheels lock the wood in place.

out a way to get the thing to work. When it comes to machines, Paul has years of experience. I have none. So if Paul has a difficult time installing a guard, what chance does a novice have? None. Most factory guards feature anti-kickback devices called pawls: These do work, if the guard is properly aligned with the blade. Needless to say, I am shopping for an after-market guard system.

In the meantime, I've equipped my saw with anti-kickback wheels, also known as hold-downs. The wheels are attached to adjustable spring-loaded tension bars, and the whole

This cabinet saw has an overarm guard on a wide extension, so it will clear sheets of plywood.

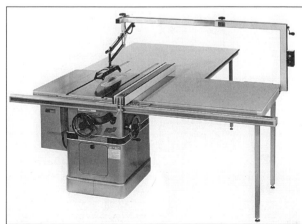

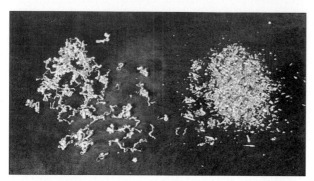

Sawdust from a rip cut tends to be long shavings, while crosscut sawdust is made of short fibers.

Flat-top grind. Best for ripping.

Alternate top bevel (ATB). Best for crosscutting

Combination blade is ATB plus flat-top rakers. For general purpose sawing.

Triple-chip grind. Best for plywood and particleboard.

assembly is attached either to an auxiliary fence (a straight hardwood board approximately the size of the table-saw fence) and then attached to the table-saw fence, or attached directly to the table-saw fence using modified metal angles (for support) and machine screws. There are three types of wheels with different rotations: clockwise only, counterclockwise only, and freewheels, which rotate in both directions. I'm right-handed, and my fence is on the right side of the blade, so I purchased wheels that rotate clockwise only, to follow the board being fed through the blade. If you are left-handed, and your fence is on the left side of the blade, you would purchase counterclockwise wheels.

I adore my anti-kickback wheels—it's like having another set of hands. Properly adjusted, the wheels hold the board tight against the fence, and since they turn only in one direction, they don't allow the board to back up and kick back. And unlike the guard that came with my saw, anti-kickback wheels can be used while milling dadoes and rabbets, and when the blade is tilted at an angle.

Sawblades

PAM: The steel blade that comes with any new table saw is worthless. Remove it at once. These blades are like the tires that come with economy cars—they are there only to get you off the lot. You will need to purchase a carbide-tipped sawblade, which will last twelve to sixty times longer than high-speed steel, depending on the quality of the blade. As with any tool, buy the best you can afford.

There are many blades to choose from, each having its own purpose. If you don't understand the difference between the blades, you will go cross-eyed trying to figure out what to buy. And if you happen to purchase your blade at a store from a salesman who doesn't know a rip blade from a laminate blade, like I did, you can end up with something on your saw that isn't doing the job. I have a blade that was sold to me as a combination blade. But the combination of what remains a mystery. Paul and I are still trying to figure out what it's supposed to be used for.

PAUL: Before continuing with the different types of sawblades, let's look at what happens to wood when it is cut by a circular blade. Think of the wood as a bundle of soda straws—when you rip the board (cut it along the length of its grain), the blade tends to bend and pull the wood fibers before cutting through, creating sawdust with long fibers. When you crosscut the board (saw it across the grain of the wood), the sawdust is made up of very small fibers. As you will see, the consistency of the sawdust has a lot to do with the way various blades are designed.

Rip blade (FTG, flat-top grind)—This blade is designed for ripping wood. It has 20 to 24 square-topped teeth, also called flat-top or chisel teeth. To allow the long-fibered sawdust generated by ripping to escape, a rip blade has plenty of large deep gullets.(If a blade with small gullets were used to rip a board, the gullets would quickly get stuffed with sawdust, slowing the cut, burning the wood, and possibly allowing the blade to become damaged from excessive heat build-up.)

Due to the large gullet size, the number of teeth on the blade are limited. The flat-top teeth on a rip blade are designed to chop through the wood, since there is very little resistance when cutting with the grain. A rip blade is not used for cutting plywoods or crosscutting. If you use it in this capacity, it will cause severe fraying and chipping, ruining your cut. It's not the gullets causing the problem, but the teeth.

Crosscut blade(ATB, alternate top bevel)— This blade is designed for crosscutting and also for milling plywood. To crosscut cleanly, you need a lot of very sharp teeth. On a crosscut blade, each tooth is ground to an angled, razor point at the tip, and every other tooth points in an alternate direction. This type of tooth configuration cuts the wood on the outside first, creating minimal grain tear-out.

A good crosscut blade has at least 60 teeth—the more teeth, the smoother the cut. The blade has very small gullets since crosscutting creates short fibers that don't fill up the gullets. Don't use a crosscut blade to rip wood. Since the small gullets can't handle long fibers, the blade will clog and burn the wood —and burn marks are difficult to sand out.

Combination blade(ATB-R, alternate top bevel-raker)— This blade can both rip and crosscut, since it has both alternate top bevel (ATB) teeth and flat-top grind (FTG) teeth. (Just to confuse you, the FTG teeth are called rakers.) The blade has both large and small gullets to accommodate the different types of sawdust created by ripping and crosscutting. This is a popular blade, because it does it all, but it won't give as clean a cut as specific-purpose blades.

TCG blade—The "TCG" stands for triple chip grind: A TCG tooth is beveled on either side, creating a wedge shape. The TCG tooth is then followed by a FTG (flat-top grind) tooth. Yes, this, too, is a combination blade, since it has two types of sawteeth. The TCG teeth cut out the center of the material, and then the FTG teeth cut the edges.

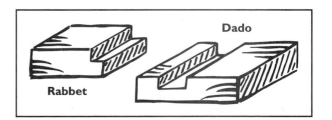

A stack dado set consists of two outer blades plus center chippers. It can be stacked to any thickness.

A carbide sawblade has teeth of tungsten carbide, which is very hard, but brittle. The carbide teeth are welded into a steel saw-plate.

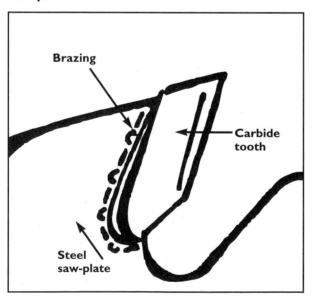

This blade is designed for cutting particle-board, fiberboard, plywood, and certain plastics (with great care). It will cut hard and soft lumber, but not as well as an ATB-R combination blade, because the gullets are small and can't accommodate long wood fibers without burning.

Sawblades come in a $1/16$-in. width, also known as a thin-kerf blade, or the standard $1/8$-in. width. A thin-kerf blade takes less power to drive, since the blade is cutting less wood than a thick blade, and therefore a thin-kerf blade requires less force to push the wood through the cut. A thin-kerf blade is used with exotics and/or expensive woods where you don't want to loose the wood to sawdust.

An $1/8$-in. wide blade is used on both cabinet and contractor's saws. Because there is more blade working than with a thin-kerf blade, you get a smoother cut. Also, a $1/8$-in. blade will last up to four times longer than a thin-kerf blade.

Dado blades—These blades are used to cut grooves in boards. If the groove has one shoulder, it's called a rabbet; if the groove has two shoulders, it's called a dado. Most projects in this book require dado blades.

There are several types of dado blades, and all can be bought either carbide-tipped or in high-speed steel. Since carbide-tipped blades are expensive, you might be tempted to purchase high-speed steel, but I recommend against it—high-speed steel blades are hard to keep sharp.

Stack dado heads— These blades consist of two circular blades plus a number of chippers and spacers. This is the most desirable of the dado blades to use. The thin spacers can be added between chippers to accurately fine-tune the dado blade to the exact width desired. Once set up, this blade will give you a flat-bottomed dado with small grooves along the bottom for excess glue. Also, it's very easy to adjust the fence, since the right side of the dado blade will line up exactly the same as a standard blade. A set of 8-in. dia. blades is preferable; there is more momentum at the outside edge to remove the wood. Since this is the type of dado set used in the book, Pam and I will show you how to stack them up once we get into the projects.

Wobble dado head—This is a blade with hubs on either side that can be turned to adjust the incline of the blade to make a wider or narrower cut; the blade can be infinitely adjusted, making it extremely accurate. But although the dado width might be accurate, getting an accurate measurement from the fence to the dado being cut is difficult. A wobble head rotates (cuts) at an angle, and you have to find the farthest point of the angle to measure from. If you purchase a wobble blade, go with a 6-in. diameter; the larger, 8-in. dia. wobble blade will slightly dish the bottom of the dado.

The bottom line—Which blades to buy: Start your blade collection with a good-quality combination carbide-tipped blade. A stack dado head set is also necessary for the projects in this book. You can use a rip, crosscut, or combination blade to achieve the same cut that a dado set will, but the time involved milling that cut is ridiculous. If you aren't convinced, try it. If you still have funds left over, or at a later date, purchase a carbide-tipped rip blade to handle all your ripping. As you become more experienced with woodworking, you will appreciate task-specific blades.

Sawblade use and care—Once you get your sawblades, you need to use them properly and take proper care of them. If you don't, you're in for a few nasty surprises.

Sawburn is one of them. There are several reasons for sawburn. If a board isn't moved through a cut quickly enough, the rotating blade keeps working the same spot, creating friction against the edge of the board. The result? Sawburn. Or the wood, not the operator, might cause sawburn. Some woods contain a large portion of pitch or resin (pine is notoriously full of pitch), which is melted by the rotating blade and deposited on or around the teeth. The pitch on the teeth will slow down the blade and increase friction, resulting in...sawburn. Another way to get sawburn is to use the wrong blade for the desired cut, for example, to use a crosscut blade for ripping. Sawdust gets packed into the gullets of the blade, adds friction to the cut, slows the blade, and guess what? Sawburn.

Likewise, cutting with a dull blade will burn the wood, since a dull blade cuts more slowly (creating friction) than a sharp one. A thin-kerf sawblade cuts quickly and will definitely burn the wood if you don't move the wood through the blade fast enough.

Make it a habit to regularly inspect and clean your sawblades. Gently scrub your blades every so often with soap and water and a soft-bristle brush. Dry the blades with a soft cloth and then lightly oil them. If necessary, you can soak the blades overnight in a solution of baking soda and water, or use carburetor or oven cleaner. Since the tannic acid in oak will eventually deteriorate carbide, you must clean your blades extra-carefully after working with it.

Always make sure to handle your blades gently—carbide is brittle and chips like mad. And never stack blades atop one another, because if the teeth contact one another, they'll chip. I hang my blades on the wall, up out of harm's way; if I double any up, I place heavy cardboard in between blades to protect the teeth. If stacking the blades flat is the only way you can store them, put them in a sturdy box with heavy cardboard in between blades.

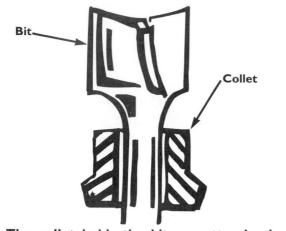

Bit

Collet

The collet holds the bit or cutter in the router (top). If you push the bit in too far (bottom), the collet can't tighten properly.

The key in the center of the base of a regular router locks the depth-of-cut adjustment. Most routers require a pair of wrenches for tightening the collet.

The router

PAUL: After you have purchased your table saw, you need to get a router, the second shop workhorse. This is my favorite tool. A router equipped with the proper bits, jigs, and fixtures can dado, rabbet, mold, and shape; it will accomplish all this accurately in repetitive cuts. The router is a tool that is easy to maintain, and it should last the home craftsperson a lifetime. If you own a good-quality router and superior table saw, you can build just about anything.

What is a good-quality router? Your router should be compact, have at least 8 amps (or a $1^{1}/_{2}$ hp motor) and accept both $^{1}/_{4}$-in. and $^{1}/_{2}$-in. shank router bits. Large-shank bits offer a greater selection of profiles and cutter dimensions, and without the capacity to hold them, you'll never fully experience what a router can produce. You can buy routers with knob handles or D-handles—it's a matter of preference. I prefer knob handles because they give better control; the balance of the machine is not compromised by a D-handle hanging off the side. However, routers with D-handles usually have dead-man switches, a trigger on the handle that, when released, cuts power to the motor.

PAM: Routers are getting bigger and more powerful each year. And unless the router is mounted in a router table, this is a hand-held power tool. First, you don't need a massive router with a bunch of jigs, certainly not right now. And how much the tool actually weighs can be a problem. When purchasing a router, pick up a few and compare weights. Some individuals prefer, and can handle, a heavier tool. I wasn't comfortable with a big bulky router; my router weighs in at about eight pounds.

PAUL: Here's how a router works: A bit shank is inserted into the collet through the bottom of the base; the depth of the bit is adjusted by moving the base up or down on the motor body. Once the depth is set, you're ready to mill.

A router bit rotates at approximately 22,000 RPM (revolutions per minute), and, quite frankly, the most intimidating thing about this little machine is turning it off and on—it's got a kick to it. If the router is on a surface when you first start it, make sure the bit won't come in contact with anything; otherwise, the bit will gouge a hole in whatever it's touching, or worse, fly off the bench—and then it's like chasing a dog that wants to attack you.

Plunge routers are similar to regular routers, but they have the extra capability of adjusting the depth of the cut by using various pre-set stops located on the base. When you have a deep cut, you have to approach it in stages; trying to mill the entire cut at once can lead to serious problems. The plunge router will easily step down the depth for each pass without having to re-adjust the base. As its name implies, it also can plunge; when you begin a cut, the bit is above the base, and with the plunge mechanism, you can drop the bit down into the work. This is handy when you are trying to cut circles and other shapes out of the center of the board, or when you are milling mortises. Generally, a plunge router is larger than a regular router, with more amperage/horsepower, and therefore is heavier and will require more physical effort to manipulate. A plunge router is a wonderful tool, but an investment that ought to be made much later, after you become more proficient in tool usage and woodworking.

Along with the router go the bits. Another reason to buy a router that takes both 1/4-in. and 1/2-in. shank bits is that the 1/2-in. shank bits don't bend easily and will eliminate chatter in most instances. Chatter is created when a router bit starts to wobble, either from vibrations set up by the motor, or by milling wood that repeatedly changes from hard to soft, such as endgrain or a knot, or anyplace where the grain changes direction. Chatter can bend, or

shear, router-bit shanks, especially 1/4-in. shanks, and will increase as the shank continues to bend during use. You can tell you're having a problem if a bit chatters on one wood, and then chatters on a completely different wood. When this happens, you must discard the bit; either it's bent, or it has lost part of its carbide cutter and is unbalanced. Continual use of a damaged bit will destroy the bearings in your router and provoke costly repairs, or ruin the router entirely, not to mention the increased safety hazards of running damaged equipment.

Great strides in machining technology have brought about the mass production of bits that only ten years ago had to be custom made. I remember going into a woodworking store in the late 1970s and having a choice of about ten

Solid-pilot router bits can follow an edge or pattern, but they may leave a burn mark.

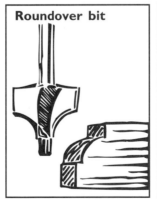
Roundover bit

Chamfer cutter

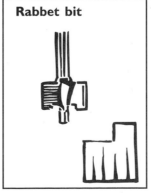
Rabbet bit

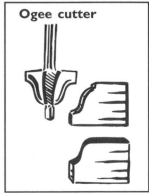
Ogee cutter

Bits with ball-bearing guides, which can follow patterns, come in a variety of configurations.

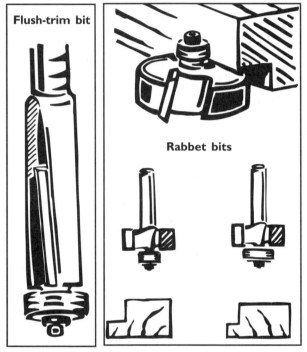

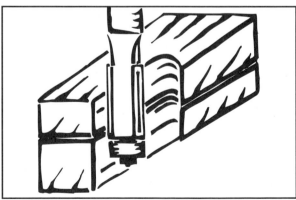

Flush trim bit in action. Ball bearing rides pattern or finished edge.

decorative profiles. Today, there are hundreds of profiles. But before you run right out and buy each router bit known to man, or worse, buy a set (this is a waste of money because some of the bits will seldom be used, once every millennium or so), consider these recommendations.

Don't buy high-speed steel bits, because they heat up and expand in use. This means that if you're cutting a slot for a shelf, the groove will become progressively larger as the bit gets hotter and expands. The shelf will fit tightly at the beginning of the cut but will be sloppy at the other end. And because of the excessive heat build-up, the bits won't stay sharp. High-speed steel bits cost more to sharpen than their value; it's cheaper to buy a new bit. The other major drawback to high-speed steel bits is that they typically employ solid pilots (as opposed to the ball-bearing guide of a carbide-tip bit). Pilots are used to follow patterns, or the edge of the board—the pilot, being an integral part of a high-speed steel bit, travels at 22,000 RPM, just like the rest of the bit. And since it is traveling so fast, the pilot will burn the edge of whatever it comes in contact with. At this point, consider your work ruined, because sanding out those burn marks is next to impossible

Always buy carbide-tip bits. These bits have the carbide tips brazed onto the cutter body. (Brazing is the soldering of two dissimilar metals, such as steel and carbide, using brass applied under very high temperatures.) Avoid solid carbide bits except when the bit is tiny, $5/_{32}$ in. or so, where it would be difficult to braze a tip onto the body.

A carbide-tip bit is manufactured to more exacting tolerances than a high-speed steel bit because carbide stays cooler in use. While a carbide-tip bit will not sharpen to as keen an edge as high-speed steel, the edge will last at least seven times longer. You can also get carbide-tipped bits sharpened for less than it cost to buy the bit, and the bit itself can be sharpened at least seven times, unless there has been extreme wear or the cutting edge has been chipped.

A carbide-tip bit has a ball-bearing guide instead of a pilot; because the guide is independent of the bit, it does not turn at 22,000 RPM like the rest of the bit, and will not burn your work. Also, by changing the bearing, you can alter the profile you're cutting.

So, what should you buy? Start with the bits that you will need to finish the projects in this book:

- A ½-in. flush trim bit. This bit is used to square the edge of a board before ripping or gluing. It's also used to make or duplicate patterns.

- A ⅜-in. rabbet bit. One with multiple bearings is nice, because you can change the width of a cut by changing the bearing. A rabbet bit is used for rabbeting in those instances when you can't pass the work through your table saw's dado blades. Maybe the board is too big, or it would be too awkward to run the work through the dado blades.

- A spiral flute bit (down-spiral) with a ½-in. shank, about 3 in. in overall length. The spiral bit is used to joint board edges and to mill dadoes and grooves. Spiral flute bits come in an up-spiral or down-spiral design. The up-spiral is used when the router is above the work; it pulls the chips up and out of the cut, which keeps the chips from packing in a dado or groove. The down-spiral is used when the router is below the work, as when it is mounted in a router table. The design of a down-spiral moves the chips away from the router motor.

The orbital jigsaw

PAUL: One of the first tools I bought when starting out was a saber saw, now called a jigsaw. As I became more adept at woodworking, I used my jigsaw less and less; it didn't cut through wood easily, plus the blade kept falling out. And when the blade was actually working, the sawdust it spewed out covered my pencil line, so I was never sure if I was on the mark or not. I finally set the saw aside.

Years later, a sales representative from a major jigsaw manufacturer visited my shop and tried to talk me into buying another jigsaw. He explained that the saw had plenty of new features that compensated for the drawbacks of the older models. I told him I wasn't interested. He left the jigsaw for me to try, anyway. I set it aside.

Not much later, a customer needed me to cut a large circle out of a piece of plywood. I used the band saw, and halfway through the cut, the blade broke. This was late on a Saturday afternoon and I didn't have a replace-

A jigsaw can cut a curve, but it's most useful for breaking down unmanageable sheets of plywood. This is a top-handled jigsaw.

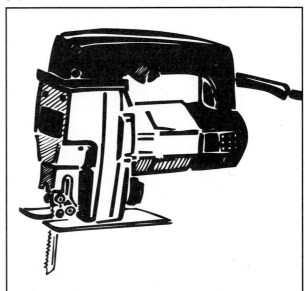

ment blade. What was I going to do? After a moment or two, I remembered the jigsaw left behind by the salesman. Since I was in a pinch, I thought I'd give it a try. Wow! The saw cut smoothly, the dust blower kept all the sawdust off the pencil line, the saw pulled itself along rather than having to be pushed, it was easy to control, and the cut was smooth as glass. Needless to say, I bought the saw when the salesman returned.

Cheaper jigsaws still have the same features as my first saw. However, if you purchase a jigsaw at the more expensive end, you will get the features of my new saw. The reason the saw works so well is due to orbital action; the saw mechanism moves the blade forward when the blade goes up, and back as the blade goes down. This draws the saw into the work and at the same times gives a cut that is extremely smooth, even in 2-in. thick, rock-hard maple.

A jigsaw is useful for breaking down large sheets of plywood and composition board, crosscutting long boards into manageable lengths, and cutting circles or other odd shapes. But for all its versatility, a jigsaw will never give a true, straight cut that can be glued to another piece. The board still needs to be sawed true on the table saw.

I prefer a top-handled jigsaw to barrel-grip models. With a barrel-grip saw, you have to use two hands—one to steer the thing and the other to hold onto the body. I prefer a top grip because it takes only one hand to hold and guide the machine. Don't bother using the tilting foot; it's inaccurate, an inherent problem with all jigsaws.

When you use a jigsaw, remember not to put your hand underneath the work in the line of cut, or you will cut off your fingers. And make sure the blade has come to a complete stop before dropping it to your side or setting it down—a running blade can puncture your leg.

If you can't afford a jigsaw at this time, then you will need to get a hand crosscut saw to break down your large boards—we'll talk about hand saws in Chapter 3. But I'm sure that after a few afternoons of sawing away on large chunks of fiberboard, you will run, not walk, to your nearest tool dealer and investigate jigsaws.

2 WHAT NOT TO BUY

Combination Machines

PAM: When I first got started, I didn't know about machines and their functions, or even which brand names were reputable. I also didn't have a bottomless bank account. Therefore, when I was advised by a friend to purchase a table saw, drill press, jointer, planer, radial arm saw, and lathe, I was more than a little discouraged. What did I need just to get started? Well, according to my friend, that would be a table saw, drill press, jointer, planer, radial arm saw, and lathe... (By the way, no one mentioned a router.)

You can either run out and purchase all these machines, or you can be sensible and start with the basics that Paul suggests and build from there. Probably the most common mistake a beginner makes is purchasing unsuitable tools—this usually happens because he or she has been conned by a slick salesman or an advertising gimmick. I happened to fall prey to the slick salesman. Let me tell you about my combination machine, and how I learned the hard way that no tool can be everything to everybody.

The particular combination machine I was looking at included a table saw, drill press, horizontal borer, sander, and lathe—everything but a board-stretcher—all in one unit. It sounded too good to be true, and it was. Little did I know that the more functions a tool has to perform, the less accurately it can perform those functions.

I was advised by several woodworkers not to purchase a combination machine, though none of them could really explain why. At issue seemed to be the amount of time required to change from one function to another. But when I asked the salesman about this, he cooled my fears with a demonstration of how easy it was to reconfigure from one mode to the next. Heck, what did I know? The machine had everything I needed and then some, so I bought it.

But it didn't take long for me to realize I had made a big mistake. For since the day the salesman came over to set up the machine for me (a task I would never have been able to accomplish alone), I have never been able to keep the machine square. What I discovered was that it took hours of fine-tuning to get a true 90-degree cut. (Truing, or squaring, a board means you cut it at exactly 90 degrees, not 89 degrees or 92 degrees.) I cannot over-stress the importance of true cuts. If you start a project making 87-degree cuts instead of 90-degree cuts, by the time you get to the end of the work you're so far out of square you will never be able to get anything to fit.

In furniture making, accuracy is extremely important, and my combination machine was anything but accurate. I ran into many problems. To begin with, the arbor (the threaded-steel rod that the sawblade is mounted on) is stationary, so to adjust blade height you move the table up and down. Drop that table just once onto the top of the motor, and the table isn't square anymore. Move the table out of 90 degrees for an angle cut, reposition it, and forget true. No one has hours to spend squaring the machine every time the table is moved. And forget using extension tables (Chapter 6) to support long, heavy boards or sheet materials—just try and build extension tables that move up and down, adjusting to the table on the saw. And without extension tables, boards can cantilever off to the side or back of the table, or be kicked back at you with great force.

I also had a problem any time I had to tilt the table to make an angle cut (miter) on the

A tilt-table saw is dangerously awkward. When cross-cutting, the offcut drops onto the blade and flies into the air. When ripping, the blade may kick the offcut back at the operator.

end of a board. During the cut, the wood was forced down onto the blade, and once past the blade, onto the board. The result? The kerf would close and pinch the blade, burning the wood and slowing or stopping the blade. What about the blade guard? Well, the guard has to be removed when the table is tilted, or it gets in the way. Crosscutting small pieces of wood was even more exciting. There was nowhere for the sawn wood to go except back down into the blade, where it was shot out of the saw like a bullet. The moral is: Never buy a tilting-table table saw. Buy a tilting-arbor table saw.

I have met people who love their combination machines and swear they are a fine investment. Either these people have a machinist background and fine-tuning their machines is no problem, or their shop space is the size of a closet and they have no choice but to use a combination machine. If you have any space for a shop, your money is best spent on individual machines that will perform one function and one function only.

Radial Arm Saws

PAUL: Although Pam had problems with her combination machine, it certainly could have been worse: She might have purchased a radial arm saw. And for those of you who don't have one yet, this is the last tool you need. Yes, that's right, the last tool.

What is a radial arm saw? It's a saw that's suspended by an arm above its table; the wood is braced against the fence and the saw is pulled across the work. Radial arm saws are meant to perform one function only: Crosscutting boards to length. All other functions with this machine are dangerous and inaccurate.

A radial arm saw is often promoted as being the only tool you'll ever need because, in addition to crosscutting, it can rip wood to width and cut angles, including compound miters. The sales pitch usually also stresses that you can use the saw as a shaper, router, hori-

The motor and blade of a radial-arm saw travel on top of the work. These saws are not accurate and are difficult to align.

zontal borer, overhead pin router, and sander. What isn't emphasized is the fact that every time you move the saw out of 90 degrees and into a different position, it will almost always be out of square when returned to its original position. And returning the saw to square is difficult, if not almost impossible. Although there are positioning stops at 45 degrees and 90 degrees intended for the quick setup of these angles, there is enough slop in the stops so the arm won't lock at the desired angle. Therefore, you really can't rely on these stops. So throw accuracy out the window.

In addition, if used incorrectly, the radial arm saw can be a dangerous tool indeed. Since your hand is between the cutter and the work, you will lose your fingers if an accident occurs. Never use a tool that has the cutter above the work unless it is absolutely the only way to accomplish the task.

When the radial arm saw is used in the rip mode, the potential danger intensifies. As the saw rips, the blade rotates up, cutting the board from the bottom to the top. The rotation of the sawblade wants to lift the work off the table, and you have to exert more force on the board to hold it down; this puts you in a vulnerable position because your reaction time will be slowed if something unexpectedly happens. (Contrast this with the ripping action of a table saw, where the blade rotates down, cutting the board from the top to the bottom, thereby pressing the work onto the table.) Remember, only the lightest touch should be necessary to move your work through a cut. If you have to force it through the cutter, and you slip, you are going to cut yourself. It's that simple.

Another problem with using the radial arm saw in rip mode is that your hand and arm are held captive between the blade, column, arm, and fence, especially at the end of the cut. Safety devices such as pushsticks can be more difficult to use in this situation and can even provoke accidents.

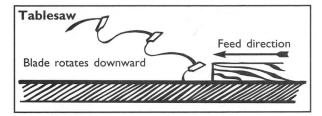
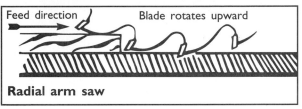

Ripping on the table saw versus ripping on the radial-arm saw

Even with a push stick, ripping brings your hand perilously close to the blade of a radial-arm saw.

The band saw is a very useful machine, but its numerous adjustments can be frustrating for the non-mechanical beginner.

Dado blades, a series of blades stacked together to cut a wide groove, are extremely hazardous when used with a radial arm saw. Dado blades really grab the wood, and if you don't exercise extreme care, the blades can shoot a board off the table and into whatever is in front of it, which might be you. If you happen to own a radial arm saw, I recommend that you use it only for crosscutting boards to length—no angle cuts, no ripping, and no dadoes.

Band Saws

PAUL: There's no doubt that a bandsaw is a useful tool, and an acquaintance of mine once asked me why I didn't recommend one for Pam. The reason is simply that most people starting up a shop are not mechanical. If a tool requires constant adjustment and alignment, it becomes frustrating to use and can lead to failure. A bandsaw has numerous drawbacks for the beginner: The blades break and take time to change, and with each blade change, the guide bearing and bushings must be realigned and adjusted. It is difficult for beginners to properly tension the blade, which if too tight, will break, and if too loose, will wander. In addition, it's a challenge to cut a straight line, since you have to freehand the wood through the blade. Sure, some bandsaws come with fences, but that doesn't solve the problem since the blade also wanders around.

If you need to cut curves and circles, you can always do it with an orbital jigsaw—in fact, I prefer the jigsaw to a bandsaw. The jigsaw gives a smoother cut and the cut width isn't limited. Nor does an orbital jigsaw require careful adjustments or mechanical wizardry. The only thing a bandsaw can do that a jigsaw can't is resaw, that is, cut the thickness of a board into two or more pieces. But resawing isn't really something a beginner should be doing anyway.

Power Miter Box

PAUL: Another tool most beginners can do without is a power miter box, also known as a chop saw. This is a great tool for trim carpenters and for woodworkers who cut a lot of precise angles, especially for picture frames and small boxes, but it can handle material only of limited width and height. All the functions accomplished by a power miter box can be performed just as precisely with a table saw—so save your money.

A power miter box is a good job-site tool, but in the workshop the table saw does the same work and a lot more.

3 OUTFITTING THE REST OF THE SHOP

Dust-Collection System

PAM: When I started setting up shop, I spent every cent I had—and then some—so there was absolutely no money left for anything, including wood. Although I had heard about dust-collection systems, I didn't know anyone who had one, or even anyone who had a good argument for getting one. A dust-collection system was considered a luxury, and besides, who can't handle a little wood dust? I had a nice shop vacuum that I had acquired earlier, and some nuisance masks (which are just that, a nuisance). I figured that was enough.

My first big project was to turn 86 replacement balusters to restore the decorative railing that wrapped around my balcony. I had to crosscut the 18-in. long blanks out of twelve 4x4x12-ft. pieces of Douglas fir. I didn't think much about the sawdust I was creating until I returned to the shop after a brief break to find a noticeable haze of wood particles adrift in the air. Realizing that breathing in these particles might not be a good thing, I put on a dust mask. I hated wearing it—the mask didn't fit tightly and caused my safety goggles to fog up. Which is worse, I asked myself, breathing wood dust or not being able to see what I'm sawing? I suffered through and kept the mask on, but as soon as the saw was turned off, and I had done a bit of cleaning with the shop vac, off came the mask. Consequently, I was still breathing in those fine wood particles, and about 24 hours later I developed a small but persistent hacking cough. If for some reason I didn't work in the shop for a few days, the cough would go away, but I didn't make that connection at the time.

In the meantime, I was going to wood-working seminars, learning more about wood, its uses, and different techniques for working it. Imagine my shock when I learned at one of Paul's wood technology lectures that all wood is toxic in one form or another. In fact, there are certain woods you wouldn't dare use without a dust-collection system. (This includes red-wood, western red cedar, myrtle, birch, willow, and black locust, to name a few, as well as fiber and particleboard, both of which contain adhesive resins that can cause severe reactions.) Paul also said that if you worked with a certain wood all the time, you would eventually develop an allergy to it. But I was also told that different types of wood could affect people in different ways, and that a wood species that might bother someone else might not bother you. Since I had milled many types of wood, and had never had a reaction (or so I thought) to any of them, my confidence returned.

After the lecture, I met some people suffering from wood-related allergies and respiratory problems. Did they have dust-collection systems? A few did, but the systems were installed after their ailments began. As I observed that the complainants were mostly old timers, who had spent their lives cooped up in dusty shops, I again felt relieved. As a relatively young person, maybe I didn't have to worry.

Wrong. The need for a dust-collection system hit me hard on the day that I asked Paul to bring over his planer. I had just purchased several different species of lumber in the rough, for future projects, and was curious as to what the wood looked like under its furry exterior. Now a planer is probably the worst when it comes to spewing out wood dust, and since I didn't own a dust-collection system at the time, we should have planed the wood outside, even though the temperature was below freezing. I

did try to strategically position the shop vac hose to collect the planer dust, but in the end the attempt was futile. You work with what you have, or, in this case, with what I didn't have—a dust collection system. Paul and I planed poplar. We planed cherry. Paul was hacking away. I was hacking away. On we planed, intent only on finishing the job and fleeing the shop. Our last board was a piece of makore (African cherry). Paul sent the board through the planer and within seconds my lungs seized up. I ran from the shop to find my dust mask, but it was too late—I sneezed continually for the next twelve hours. I had finally found the wood that I couldn't work with

What price do you put on your respiratory system? Obviously, there's none high enough. And once the damage is done, well, it's done. As I found out, a dust-collection system is not a luxury, it's a necessity. It took me two years to figure this out, two years of listening to—but not really believing—older woodworkers saying they wished they had added a system years ago.

Now, if the respiratory problems caused by working wood don't impress you, then perhaps the fire hazards created by sawdust will. Did you know that when you add static electricity to sawdust, the dust can build up to a flash point? Believe it. Here's how this translates: If fine sawdust seeps into the electrical boxes in your shop, and for some reason there is a loose connection, you have the potential to create a fire. Additionally, it possibly could be the type of fire you don't notice until it's too late. The same thing can happen with your tools, sanders in particular. If sawdust accumulates inside the motor, when you turn the motor on the spark created by the brushes can ignite the sawdust. Piles of sawdust left lying around can also ignite by spontaneous combustion. Now, I know you need a rather big pile of sawdust for this to happen, but some people don't throw anything away. If you have a dust-collection system, you can help eliminate these problems.

I don't know the size of your shop, or your pocketbook, but I'll take you through the basics, and then it's up to you to research the systems and buy the one that is right for you. Owning a shop vac is fine, but it can't do what a dust-collection system is designed to do.

Types of dust-collection systems—Currently there are three types of systems available (four, if you want to count overhead air-cleaning systems). I'm sure in the future new systems will evolve as the importance of dust collection becomes clearer to all involved.

The first type, and the one that I own, is called a one-stage collector or a single-stage blower-and-bag system. These machines have two collection bags, one on top of the other; the hose outlet(s) is positioned in front of the motor. The debris is collected through the inlet(s) and then deposited into the bags; the larger chunks fall into the bottom bag, yet both bags act as a filter before exhausting the air back into the shop. You should empty the bottom bag when it is about half-full for maximum filter capacity.

The second type of dust-collection system is a two-stage collector, or two-stage blower-and-bag collector. This looks like a large metal shop vac with a car air filter on top, with a bag

A cyclone collector is the most efficient machine for controlling wood dust, but it's also the most expensive. The one-stage machine is adequate for most home shops.

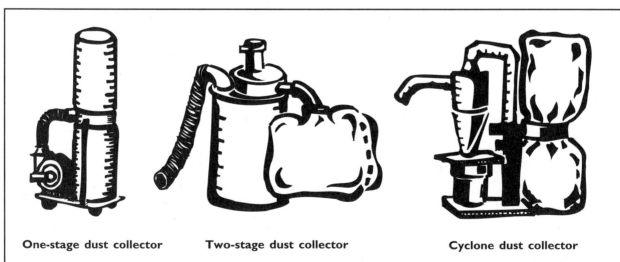

One-stage dust collector   Two-stage dust collector   Cyclone dust collector

attached to that. The debris is collected through a hose in the top and deposited into the metal canister, then the air is exhausted through the blower and into an air filter bag before returning to the shop. A two-stage collector can do the job with greater efficiency, since the larger particles are left behind in the canister, and the air filter bag only has to capture the fine dust. However, a two-stage system will cost at least a couple of hundred of dollars more than a one-stage collector.

The third type of dust-collection system is called a cyclone pre-collector, or just a cyclone. The cyclone is a scaled-down version of the collectors used in industry. The debris enters into a large metal collector, where the spiraling air action causes most of the dust and chips to fall to a bin below the cyclone. The air is then filtered upward through a hose, past a blower, and into large filter bags where the finest dust is captured before the air enters the shop again. Efficient? You bet. These huge machines will suck wallpaper off the walls. However, this is the most expensive of the systems and is really meant for the professional shop, where many machines are run on a day-to-day basis.

As with any machine, you have to determine how much space you can dedicate to it, and a dust-collection system can eat up a lot of space. There are small single-stage systems that will fit underneath a bench, and if you have a small shop, that might work for you, but the system isn't going to capture a lot of dust. The larger single-stage and two-stage collectors usually need a committed area since rolling them around the shop can get awkward. In this case, you set the dust collection machine out of the way, or as much out of the way as you can, and then run a hose from the dust collection system to the machine you are using.

I looked at all of the systems before getting my one-stage collector. I would have preferred a two-stage system but finances dictated otherwise. When my collection system arrived,

it included plans to retrofit the one-stage into a modified two-stage with the addition of a metal trash can and a few hose clamps and hose adapters. Though the trash can makes the system easy to empty (you just pop off the lid), and protects the impeller from getting beat up by large chunks of wood, it also takes up more room and decreases the system's air-flow capacity, meaning my collector lost quite a bit of suction. Here's the bottom line; if you want a two-stage system, then spend the money and get a two-stage system, don't try to modify your one-stage system.

After stressing the urgency of dust collection, I really don't suggest that you run right out to your local salesperson, who is trained to sell you what is right for the company's bank account, not your shop. After reading several articles about collection systems, I went though all my catalogs and looked at the differences among one-stage collectors. These boil down to amps, number of outlets, bag size, CFM (cubic-feet-per-minute), air flow, wiring, overall size, weight, and sound rating. You are the only one who can decide what is right for you, since you know the size of your shop and how much you can spend.

Most of the time you will be able to add adapters to the hoses on the system to interface with your tools; in other instances, you will have to build custom hoods to adapt to particular activities, such as lathe turning, hand-held routing, and sanding. For these, you might want to check out air-exchange units, which work by completely exchanging the air in your shop.

Keep your dust-collection system close at hand to help with the overall dust problem, and if you're in a really dusty situation, by all means put on a dust mask. A good mask is NIOSH/MSHA (National Institute for Occupational Safety and Health, and Mine Safety and Health Administration) approved and is usually made of a heavy felt-type material, not just thin paper. Look for these at your paint

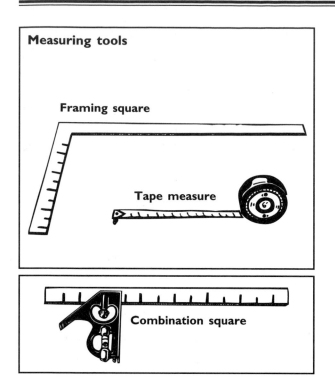

Measuring tools

Framing square

Tape measure

Combination square

To check a square for square, draw a line from the edge of a board, then flip the square over and draw another line. If the lines are parallel, the square is square. If it's not square, you'll see the error.

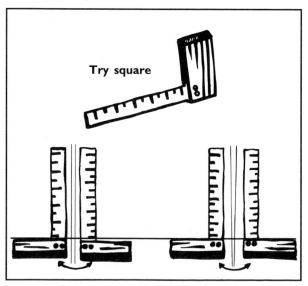

Try square

store or in woodworking mail-order catalogs. Or, if you already have a respiratory disease, invest in a dust helmet. The helmet comes with a full hood assembly that is pulled down over your face and secured about the neck (you'll look like a beekeeper). A hose from the helmet attaches to the air filter/battery pack worn on the waist; air is sucked through the filter unit and directed up the hose into the helmet, thus supplying clean, filtered air to the user. This might seem like overkill, but some people can't handle any wood dust.

Between a dust-collection system and a good dust mask, you will be giving yourself adequate protection to enjoy woodworking for years to come.

The Toolbox

PAM: Now that you've got the big stuff—table saw, router, orbital jigsaw, dust-collection system—you'll need to get the rest of the tools that are essential to woodworking. Paul has practically every tool known to man; he's been collecting for quite a while. I had...actually, I wasn't sure what I had. I had inherited a tool room along with my house, and it was full of interesting stuff, most of which I couldn't identify. Thankfully, it did get me started. As time went on, I learned the names of many of the obscure items. However, since I really didn't know what I had, or needed, I tended to purchase plenty of items that I would use only once, or worse, never use at all—I admit it, I went a little wild with all the gadgets that are supposed to make woodworking easier. Here is a list of the tools you will regularly use, and thus need, in the shop.

Tools of measurement—Get a tape measure, but not an expensive one (you won't be using it much). You will need a 6-inch try square, and/or framing square, to check if your work is square. Check that your square is square as shown in the drawing. If it's not square, get rid of it. (Try to check the square before you buy the tool.) You'll also need a combination square, for transferring measurements. You will use your combination square a lot, so get a good one. Paul and I will teach you how to use a combination square to transfer measurements, which is the most accurate way to go about it. For many measurements, we will be using a story pole, which is just a long, thin piece of wood that has been scribed at certain lengths for reference. Sound confusing? I've got news for you, you're going to love it since you don't have to keep peering at all those little lines on the tape or ruler.

Pencils—Use a pencil, not a pen, to transfer all those measurements, in case you need to erase. Get yourself a box of pencils, and scatter them around the shop. Even so, they will probably always be across the shop when you need them.

Clamps—No doubt about it, you'll need a lot of these. But there are so many different clamps on the market, which ones do you buy? You can never have too many clamps. The only clamp I would avoid is the C-clamp; the body of the clamp limits its clamping depth, and it won't span distances, which is fine if you are only going to clamp small boards together.

Spring clamps: These clamps are quick and easy to position, but don't depend on them for gluing wood since you can't adjust how much pressure is being applied to the glueline.

Bar clamps/quick action clamps: These clamps are the most common types used in the shop. They come in various sizes ranging from short to long, with different jaw depths. The top clamping fixture is stationary, fixed to the bar; the bottom part, which includes the screw, slides up or down the bar, allowing for quick adjustment and tightening. You will need at least four 6-in. or 12-in. bar clamps and at least four 18-in. bar clamps to start, but buy as many as you can afford since these are the clamps you'll use the most. Don't buy anything longer than an 18-in. bar clamp; beyond that, you lose pressure because the bar starts to bend, which brings us to the next clamp.

Pipe clamps: These clamps substitute a pipe for the bar and the clamping fixtures are reversed—the tightening screw is located at the top of this clamp, while the bottom fixture slides along the pipe. Because the clamp fixtures are purchased separately from the pipe, the pipe can be any length you choose. When you have to span a great width or length, these

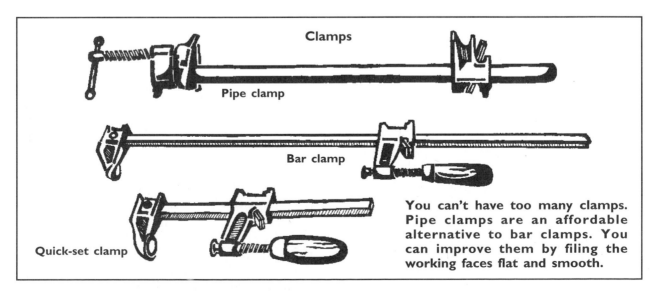

Clamps

Pipe clamp

Bar clamp

Quick-set clamp

You can't have too many clamps. Pipe clamps are an affordable alternative to bar clamps. You can improve them by filing the working faces flat and smooth.

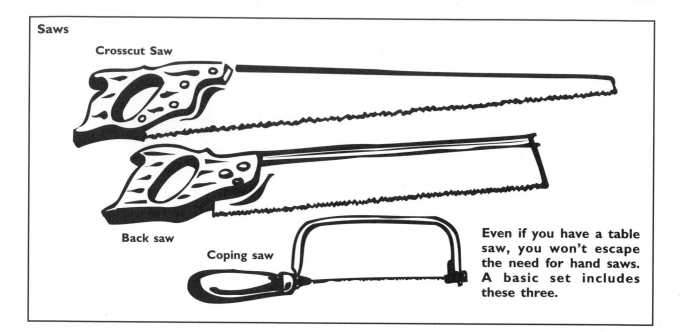

Saws

Crosscut Saw

Back saw

Coping saw

Even if you have a table saw, you won't escape the need for hand saws. A basic set includes these three.

are the clamps of choice for strength and economy. The only problem with pipe clamps is that they are heavy and clumsy when clamping small work. You will need at least seven or eight ¹/₂-in. pipe clamp fixtures, with lengths of 48-in. pipe.

Handsaws—You'll need several saws to get started. A back saw is a must; I use my back saw more than any other handsaw. This saw has a long, rectangular blade with a thick piece of metal along its back which keeps the blade rigid for accurate cuts. The blade is designed for crosscutting and is used for cutting miters, squaring the ends of boards, forming tenons, and anything else requiring exact cuts. Back saws come in two sizes: The large one is known as a miter saw, the small one is called a dovetail saw. While a dovetail saw is easier to control than a miter saw, the depth of the cut is limited.

You should have a coping saw—a saw with a very thin blade stretched across a U-shaped frame. This small saw is used to cut out the backside of molding to make it fit better, and, because of its flexible blade, is great for cutting odd shapes such as scallops and circles.

When you really have to go at it, a large crosscut saw is invaluable. Get one that has a 10- or 12- point blade (point = teeth per inch). Stay away from plastic handles, which signal a cheap saw.

If you purchase good-quality saws, and treat them respectfully, they should last a lifetime. Keep a saw in shape by taking it in for sharpening as soon as the teeth show signs of dulling.(You know your saw's getting dull when it becomes harder and harder to cut wood with it.)

Chisels—Eventually chisels will become an important part of your toolbox, but it takes time to learn how to use them correctly, and sharpening a chisel is an art in itself. There are plenty of chisels on the market, but the only type to be concerned with right now is the bench chisel. The bench chisel has a shallow bevel at the end of the blade, and beveled edges on either side of the blade. Since the shallow front bevel can be sharpened to a razor edge, all that is usually required to remove wood is hand pressure, or a gentle tap with a mallet. The bench chisel is used to clean out the little ridges left by inconsistent router depth or poorly aligned dado blades, to cut mortises for hinges, and to pare small amounts of wood from the shoulders of tenons to make the tenons fit perfectly. Be sure to look for handles that will stand up to a wood mallet, which is used to strike the chisel. To start with, you don't need that many chisels—look for $1/8$-in., $1/4$-in., and $1/2$-in. blades, or you can buy a set.

Sharpening your chisel—A chisel's cutting edge must be honed to obtain a keen edge. You will need two items: a waterstone and a honing guide. I use a waterstone because it cuts faster and more uniformly than an oilstone. A combination (double-sided) 1000/6000-grit waterstone is just fine for honing: the 1000-grit side is to form the edge; the 6000-grit side is to polish the edge. A waterstone needs to be soaked in water (submerge the entire stone) for about five minutes before use. The water acts as a lubricant and also keeps the microscopic metal shavings from becoming embedded in the stone. A simple honing guide helps keep the correct angle on the chisel's beveled edge.

To adjust the honing guide to match the bevel of the chisel, place the chisel between the jaws on the guide, and then place the guide on the stone; move the chisel up or down between the guide jaws until the chisel's beveled edge

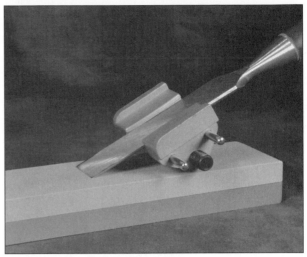

A honing guide holds the chisel at the correct angle while you draw it across the sharpening stone.

rests flat on the stone; tighten the guide jaws to lock the chisel into position. To hone the chisel's edge, push down (gently, this doesn't take must pressure) on the guide and chisel and make one long stroke down the length of the stone. At the end of the stroke, lift the chisel off the stone and reposition for another stroke. Don't drag the chisel back down the stone to the starting position, or you'll dull the edge. Make repeated passes at the stone until the chisel is razor-sharp, which could take anywhere from 10 to 12 passes. Wipe your stone off before you put it away.

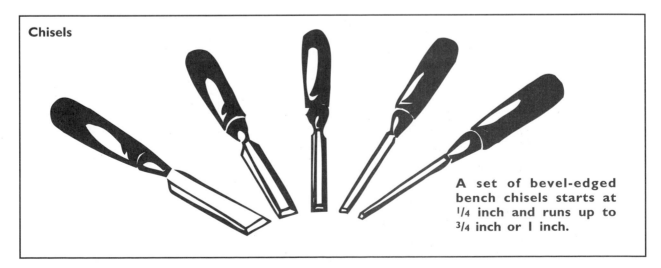

Chisels

A set of bevel-edged bench chisels starts at $1/4$ inch and runs up to $3/4$ inch or 1 inch.

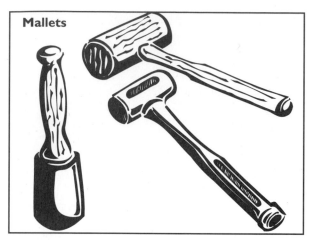

A carving mallet, left, is for driving chisels and carving tools into the wood. A wooden mallet, top, or a plastic dead-blow mallet, center, helps coax parts together.

Wooden mallets—When you need to coax your joints together, do so with a wooden mallet or a dead-blow mallet, never with a steel hammer. The difference between a dead-blow mallet (which is usually filled with lead shot) and a wooden mallet is that a dead-blow mallet is heavier and will do the coaxing with more oomph. Also, a dead-blow mallet will seldom leave a mark, whereas a wooden mallet will dent the wood if you accidentally hit it with the mallet edge.

Odds 'n ends—You'll need a utility knife or a pocket knife made with good-quality steel that will hold an edge, and a paint scraper; Paul uses a pocket knife and carries it with him at all times. I prefer a utility knife. When the blade gets dull, either flip the blade over and use the other edge, or replace it—it doesn't get any easier than that. Either one is fine, as long as you're comfortable carving, scraping, whittling, cutting, and scribing with it.

You'll also need a paint scraper to get rid of any dried, excess glue from the wood. Choose whatever size scraper fits comfortably in your hand.

To make servicing your machinery easier, stock your toolbox with an array of wrenches, including box wrenches (left), T-handle Allen wrenches (center), and adjustable wrenches (right).

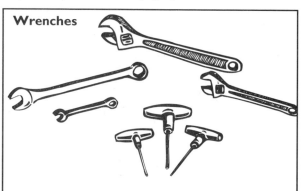

Wrenches—Since woodworking involves machinery, and there will be times when you need to work on your machines, you need to have the right tools to do the job. A set of combination open-end/box-end wrenches, one large and one small adjustable-end wrench, and a set of Allen (hex) wrenches, preferably with t-handles, will do the job. I've taken apart many a machine with my adjustable-end wrenches, and I'm here to tell you that a set of combination open-end/box-end wrenches would have made the job infinitely easier.

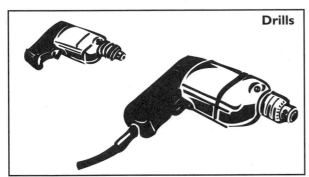

Whether corded or cordless, choose a drill that fits your hand comfortably.

Portable power drills and drill bits

PAM: You don't need a huge industrial drill, since "the bigger the better" doesn't apply to drills. Later on, you probably will purchase a drill press, either a floor or bench model. However, a portable power drill will go where your drill press can't, and in the long run you will use a portable power drill more than a drill press.

You can purchase a basic portable drill that will plug into the AC current of your shop; some of the standard, no-frills drills even come with a reverse feature—nice, but not necessary. You can dig deeper into your wallet and purchase a battery-powered portable drill, which works off a rechargeable battery inside the housing. These are expensive drills, and you pay for the extra features that come with them. If you intend to use your drill to drive screws, then you need a drill with a clutch: The clutch creates resistance, which prevents the bit from spinning the head off a screw or stripping out the threads the screw just cut in the wood. Also, a more expensive drill will come with a keyless chuck: Insert the bit and turn on the drill, which tightens the chuck, reverse loosens the chuck. Weight is a factor when looking at any drill, some are so heavy they aren't comfortable to use after any length of time.

Along with your drill, you'll need brad-point and twist bits. Bradpoint bits are essential for woodworking, since they are designed to facilitate the cutting of wood fibers. To understand a brad point, you need to follow the bit through a cut: The needle-like point is the first part of the bit to contact the wood; its self-centering nature keeps the bit from wandering all over the wood. Following the needle-like point, the outside spurs cut the circumference of the hole—the reason the outside of the bit cuts first is to reduce grain tear-out from the edge of the hole. Finally, the inside cutting edge makes contact and cuts the inside of the hole. Because of its design, a brad point bit won't cut metal. Always buy drill bits in a set;

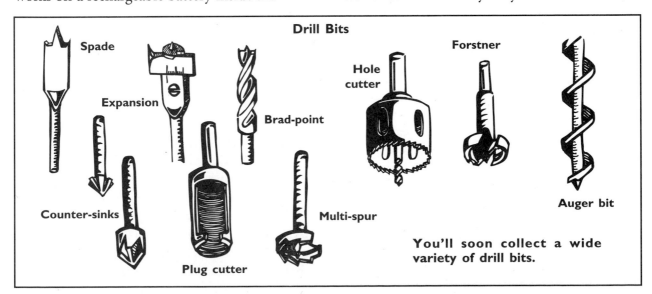

Drill Bits

Spade

Expansion

Brad-point

Counter-sinks

Plug cutter

Multi-spur

Hole cutter

Forstner

Auger bit

You'll soon collect a wide variety of drill bits.

Tapered bits and countersink bits make pilot holes for wood screws.

it's cheaper, and you'll have an assortment of sizes to choose from. The optimal set of brad points to purchase would be made of high-speed steel, and include bits from $1/8$-in. through $1/2$-in. in $1/16$-in. graduations. It might sound like a lot of bits, but in the end you'll probably use every one of them.

You will also need an array of twist bits. These bits gently taper toward the center, allowing them to start cutting at the center and then gradually toward the edge of the hole. This design is ideal for drilling metal without excessive heat buildup. In woodworking, a twist bit is used to chase holes (redrilling a hole to a larger size). An optimal set would consist of bits from $1/16$ in. through $1/2$ in. in $1/16$-in. graduations.

There are some specialty bits most beginners won't need, at least not right away. Forstner bits clog and burn easily and are difficult to keep sharp. They are also quite expen-

Screws are classified by the type of head. From left, flat-head wood screw, round-head, and oval head. Drywall screws and construction screws, right, have steep, sharp threads and Phillips-style heads.

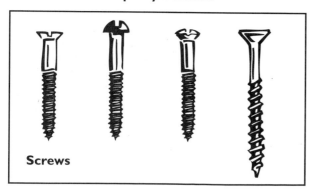

Screws

sive. Instead of cutting, spade bits work by scraping and tearing out the wood. A spade bit can wobble when drilling, making a larger, and sometimes oval, hole that will not give a proper fit or look. A spade bit is used primarily in carpentry, to drill holes for door knobs and bolts.

Fasteners

PAM: Fasteners for woodworking may be screws, nails, staples, or bolts. In fine woodworking, the preferred way to join wood to wood is with glue, but when you need extra strength or can't use glue for some reason, wood screws are used. You can identify a wood screw by its deep, sharp threads; a machine screw has shallow, tiny threads. When the screw will be hidden, you can use drywall screws; because of their sharp threads and steep spiral, drywall screws will cut their own threads and are hence self-tapping (you don't have to predrill the hole). Use brass wood screws if fasteners will be visible. Pre-drill the hole with steel screws (drill a pilot hole, sink a steel screw the same size as the brass screw that is to be used, back it out, and then set the brass screw). You do this because brass is very soft, and if you try to set brass screws in certain hardwoods, you will twist the head right off. Although pre-drilling may seem like a lot of trouble, it's nothing compared to trying to remove a headless brass screw that's been sunk into the wood.

As you wander up and down the aisle at the hardware store, you will notice that screws have different types of heads. Flat-head screws are intended for countersinking below the surface; once below the surface, they can be covered with a plug. Round-head screws are used for a decorative effect when a smooth appearance is not desired. Oval-head screws are used for mounting hardware, especially hinges, since oval-heads are made to mate snugly in machined holes. Whenever you buy screws, buy them by the box; you can never have enough.

Power sanders and abrasives

PAM: There are many hand-sanding gadgets available—blocks, sticks, flexible sanding curves, and wedges—but a block of wood or a wooden dowel will do essentially the same thing. I use a small rubber sanding block to get into tight places, and a 9-in. drywall sander with a handle for larger areas. When I need to sand molding, I wrap a piece of sandpaper around a wooden dowel that fits the profile of the molding and use that.

Hand-sanding is a long, laborious process, and quite possibly, after a few projects, you are going to wonder if there isn't a better way. There is. However, you will still have to do some hand-sanding—there's just no way around it.

I adore my portable belt sander. I would not, could not, live without it. It's relatively small, with a 3-in. wide by 18-in. length belt size, convenient when I've needed to hold the sander over my head to work on ceilings during restoration jobs. When clamped to the bench, it also works as a stationary sander.

There are two things to know about a belt sander. First, using one requires skill. You have to float the sander across the wood, being careful to keep the belt flat. If you apply pressure at the front or rear of the belt, or tip the machine even slightly to the side, the belt will create ridges you will never get out. It took me a few months to get the feel of my sander. Second, a belt sander is not a finishing sander. Its purpose in life is to knock down rough surfaces or to level out uneven surfaces. As with any power tool, purchase yours from a reputable woodworking tool manufacturer. I wouldn't recommend a belt sander using a belt smaller than 3x18 in. or one larger than 4x24 in. Remember, this is a portable power tool; the bigger the belt sander is, the heavier and more awkward it will be to use, and the more money you will shell out for the belts (due to size).

Random-orbit sanders are for finish sanding. They smooth the wood but don't remove much material.

If you do get a belt sander, make sure it has a dust collector attached to it, since these machines make a lot of dust.

When you buy your belt sander, also purchase an abrasive cleaning stick. This looks like a large rectangular eraser and is used on the belt, while running, to clean the loaded sandpaper. You can tell your belt needs cleaning when it quits cutting.

For finish sanding, a random orbit sander can't be beat. While its sanding disc revolves in a circle, the sander moves the disc in an oval orbit, producing a completely random sanding action. These sanders are very powerful and can quickly remove wood, leaving a scratch-free

Belt sanders, below, can remove a lot of material in a hurry.

surface—no matter in which direction you sand. And if you do have visible scratches on the surface, then use the next finer paper.

There are three types of random orbit sanders. In a right-angle machine, the motor is located in a handle that is attached to the side of the sander. An in-line sander has its motor housed in the sander; the in-line sander is better balanced and is easier to control than a right-angle sander. The third type of sander, the palm grip type, is a small, lightweight, in-line sander that is best used for fine finish sanding.

Abrasives (sandpaper)

PAUL: The "sand" in sandpaper is a misnomer. Sand may have been used in developing this product way back when, but sand is too soft to effectively smooth wood. The term "abrasive" is more accurate, encompassing a variety of materials. In ascending order of durability, these materials are: garnet, aluminum oxide, silicon carbide, and zirconia alumina. We'll come back to these later.

Abrasive backing materials come in weights from A through X. A-weight is the thinnest (lightest), and X is the thickest (heaviest). A-weight paper is the stuff that is found in most hardware stores and home centers.

Current technology has been able to produce distinct grits, from 12 to 12,000. Most of these grits are graded by passing them through a screen, that is, 60-grit abrasive will pass though a screen with 60 holes per linear inch, which is actually 3,600 holes per square inch, but will not pass through the next finer screen, 80 holes per linear inch. After the grit has been sized, it is applied to the backing with hide glue (for its flexibility) or resins (for strength), or a combination of both. The abrasive is spread on the backing in one of two ways. If it is spread sparingly (40 to 60 percent coverage), the abrasive paper is said to have an open-coat (labeled on some papers as "OC"). Open-coat abrasives cut fast but clog easily, requiring fre-

quent cleaning with abrasive cleaning blocks. If the abrasive totally covers the backing, the paper is closed-coat ("CC"). This type of paper can be used with water or oil as a lubricant and is used, by hand, to polish out the final finish.

Choosing the right abrasive—Garnet is a fast-cutting mineral that fractures easily when sanding, creating extremely sharp edges. I don't recommend garnet abrasive for power sanding; the abrasive wears down so fast that it is a waste of money. It is better used in hand-sanding. And because of its sharp edges, it doesn't leave as smooth a surface as aluminum oxide or silicon carbide.

Aluminum oxide abrasive is available in all forms: sheets, disks, drums, cords, and belts. Aluminum oxide is not as sharp as garnet and doesn't fracture; however, it is very durable, making it ideal for power sanding, since the machine speed compensates for its slower cutting characteristics.

Silicon carbide wet/dry abrasive cuts faster and lasts longer than both aluminum oxide and garnet. Consequently, it is considerably more expensive, but it is superior for working the final surface by hand and is thin enough to allow the most minute imperfections to be felt. You can purchase silicon carbide paper in grits ranging from 80 to 1200.

Alumina zirconia is the most durable, long lasting, fast-cutting abrasive available. Because the backing is very thick and stiff and the grit is so coarse (24 to 80 grit), it is only produced in belts and discs for large sanders. Although it's more expensive than all the other abrasives, it has no equal in its surface-cutting characteristics and the ability to withstand heat and pressure.

PAM: A word about aluminum oxide cloth-backed abrasives. Professionals have used cloth-backed abrasives for years, and finally it has been made available to the consumer. You can purchase cloth-backed abrasives in sheets and for belt sanders, random-orbit finishing sanders, and many other sanders as well. For years I used that flimsy paper-backed stuff and hated sanding. I still can't say I'm very fond of it, but with cloth-backed abrasives, sanding had become bearable. Not only do cloth-backed abrasives last longer, they're easier to maneuver since the cloth doesn't tear easily. Once you use cloth-backed abrasives, you will never touch paper-backed again.

PAUL: In your inventory you should have 100-, 120-, and 150-grit abrasives, paper- or cloth-backed, sheets or belts, depending on what equipment you'll be using. For finishing, stock 220-grit up to 400-grit abrasives, wet and dry, for rubbing out the final coat.

You can build useful sawhorses with lengths of 2x4 and commercial sawhorse brackets, which come in a variety of styles.

Sawhorses

PAM: Sawhorses have an infinite number of uses. You'll need them to build the extension tables for the table saw (Chapter 6) and also to build the workbench (Chapter 7). You can buy sawhorses, or build them. I used sawhorse brackets and 2x4s, followed the instructions that came with the brackets, and had my sawhorses together in less than an hour. I made the legs 31 in. long, and the top 23 in. long. You don't need fancy sawhorses, just something strong enough to support whatever it is you have to hold.

You can make sawhorses any length you like.

The bottom line

PAM: Do you need all this stuff? Yes. The power sanders are about the only thing that can come later. You don't have to buy top of the line—flea markets and garage sales are great places to find tools. I own a power screwdriver, it's a great tool, but a manual screwdriver will do the same thing. There will be other tools that you will be adding to your repertoire once you become more familiar with woodworking, but for now, this should be sufficient.

Shop wiring

PAM: I admit it, I'm an electrical illiterate. I've always assumed you plug it in, turn it on, and go. That, in fact, is what I did, even though I had all this electrical equipment and only one outlet on the other side of the room.

If you're anything like me, I know you can hardly wait to get started on your first project, but there are a few things you should know before you hit the ON switch of your saw. You should know the electrical loads of your machines. And what about that extension cord? Is it big enough to handle the electrical load? Paul is going to explain the electrical stuff, which is not to say that you are going to become an electrician, only that you are going to become an informed consumer.

PAUL: In Pam's home, which was built just after the turn of the century, electricity is conducted by wires the size of hairs and a service panel (breaker box) that can handle only 60 amps. While this was fine at a time when there were few electrical appliances, it's dangerous in a woodshop. Pam's lights would dim when running a tool—a sure warning that she was drawing too much current and overloading the circuit, which could have ruined the tool's motor or even started an electrical fire.

Most shop areas, garages, and basements have only one or two electrical outlets. As a woodworker acquires more tools, he or she finds that more outlets are needed in other locations throughout the shop. An individual might try to tie into the existing electrical outlet either by connecting new wires to the switch or outlet and running new wire along or through the wall, or by adding a multiple plug device to the existing plug outlet. As more outlets are added, the circuits can be overloaded, which will create a potential for electrical hazard (shock) or fire. It is best to consult an electrician before you run into trouble.

Your portable power tools (router, belt sander, drill, jigsaw), require one 15-amp circuit (as long as you won't be running all the tools at the same time); these circuits are usually accessed by outlets around the wall. Stationary machines such as table saws and lathes each require a 20-amp circuit of their own, called a dedicated circuit. The electrical motors that power these machines draw an increased amount of electricity during start up. Fifteen-amp circuits would be constantly tripping breakers, overheating motors, and possibly causing fires.

If you are going to use a number of large stationary tools, or your shop is a considerable distance from the service panel, you need a 60-amp sub-panel. The sub-panel will allow one circuit for portable power tools (wall outlets), a circuit for the table saw, a circuit for lighting, and other circuits for future tool acquisitions. The wiring from a sub-panel to the electrical outlets is shorter than if run from the outside service panel; a shorter run creates less resistance, allowing more current to be available to efficiently power the motors. Individual breakers can be shut off for maintenance on plugs, switches, and possible future additional wiring needs. All the breakers in the sub-panel can be turned off, and the sub-panel door locked, to control who uses the tools in the shop—a good safety feature if children are around.

Extension cords—Extension cords serve a useful purpose by connecting tool cords to electrical outlets; it never fails, no matter how long the tool cord is, it never quite reaches the outlet. Yet extension cords can create very serious safety hazards. Extension cords can accumulate on the shop floor and act like trip wires. They may not have a ground wire or grounded plug. Also, extension cords increase the distance between your tool and the outlet by the length of the cord; this can decrease voltage to the tool, making the tool run less efficiently and risking possible damage to the motor. An extension cord with too small a wire gauge for the tool being used can also create a voltage drop, which can damage the tool and lead to an electrical fire. There will always be a circumstance when an extension cord is needed. So pay attention to the extension cord length and gauge in relation to your work area and the tools the cord is used for, and make sure the wire gauge is the correct size to handle the electrical load.

About grounding....

Run wiring in below-grade areas, such as basements, through conduit. In most areas, this is code. In basements and shops with water seepage, water can create a fatal shock even with traditional grounding. What is grounding? To understand grounding, you need a bit of background as to how electricity gets into your house. Three wires are run from the electrical source (pole) to the house (via the service panel) and then to every outlet and switch in the house: Two hot wires carry the electricity and the third wire is the ground. The ground wire is always green, or green with different colored stripes, or bare. The two hot wires can be any color except white, green or bare. At the pole, the ground wire is either attached to a steel rod and buried in the ground, or run through a galvanized steel rod and attached to the street side of a cold water main. The ground wire is connected to each electrical outlet or switch and is never interrupted (cut); the ground wire is continuous from the pole, throughout the house, back to the ground. In the event of a short circuit, the ground wire diverts the excess electricity and runs it into the ground. The ground wire is important when related to the tools you are using. If the tool isn't grounded, or the outlet isn't grounded and a short occurs, then you become the ground. At the very least, you can be shocked; the very worst, you can be killed. The amount of shock depends on the surface you are standing on, your physical condition, and the condition of your skin at the point of contact. If you are standing on a rubber mat, or dry floor, you experience very little shock; if you are standing on a damp surface (basement), you can receive a severe shock; if you are standing in water, you would receive a maximum shock, or death. Make sure all electrical circuits are grounded and that the grounding prongs on cords attached to tools are not missing. Most portable power tools made today are double insulated and have cords without ground prongs. Double insulated means that there are two layers of plastic between you and the motor, and electricity can't travel through all that plastic if the tool shorts out. A double-insulated tool is designed to keep you from becoming the ground in case of a short. However, an extra margin of safety can be obtained by using ground fault circuit interrupter plugs (GFCI).

To prevent electrical shock, replace your outlets with GFCI receptacles. In my shop, I mount GFCI outlets in insulated (non-metallic) exterior boxes and suspend them from the ceiling and over my benches, with armored cable so that they can be easily reached. This eliminates those extension cords (which are so easy to trip over) and keeps my power-tool cords out of the way of the machines.

Ground fault circuit interrupter

The identification plate on a motor gives its voltage rating and tells how much starting current (amperes) it will draw.

EXTENSION CORD SELECTOR
For cords 50 feet or less, at 110 volts

Current	Wire gauge
10 amps	16 gauge
13 amps	16 gauge
18 amps	14 gauge
25 amps	12 gauge
30 amps	10 gauge

The lower the wire gauge number, the heavier the wire and the more current it can carry.

The amount of current (electrical power) that drives the motor is governed by the length and size of the wire that electricity travels through. The smaller the wire, and the longer it is, the more resistance is built up and the less current (electricity) can flow. The extension cord chart gives you the proper size and length of the wire to use with extension cords.

Lighting

PAUL: Lighting is critically important. If you can't see what you're doing, you're going to get hurt. To properly light a shop, use 80-watt fluorescent cool white bulbs. The lights should be placed along the ceiling so there aren't any harsh shadows cast by the tools, or you. Fluorescent fixtures and bulbs should be recessed into the ceiling and covered with a diffuser. If this is not possible, plastic sleeves can be purchased to surround each fluorescent tube; if a tube is broken for any reason, the glass will not shatter all over the shop—and you. Task lighting is used to illuminate the cutting areas of the major tools and workbench areas where overhead lighting will not eliminate shadows.

All your lights should be run on a 15-amp circuit that's separate from your tools. This way, if a tool blows a fuse, you won't lose your lighting. However, you can overload a circuit if you have too many lights on it. To avoid an overload (and a blackout), add the wattages of all the lights in the shop, just as if they were all on at the same time; divide that total by 115 volts—this will give you the number of amps you are drawing. The optimum amperage should be 13 amps or below. On a 15-amp circuit, you should allow 15 to 20 percent for possible electrical surges to avoid blackouts.

4 SHOP SAFETY

Work Safely!

PAM: Everything plugged in and grounded? I hope so, because the last thing you want to worry about is getting shocked or blowing up a machine or starting an electrical fire.

Think before you proceed—This is Paul's favorite saying, and after hearing it a zillion times, it's become mine. I've read tons of articles about safety in the shop, and most of them have scared me to death. Safety is a big concern of mine. People can get seriously hurt in a shop if they don't know what they're doing. I'll start with the basics. Bad habits are hard to break, so get into good habits before the bad ones form.

Always wear safety glasses—You want maximum comfort when it comes to safety glasses. If you don't care for the ones sold at the hardware store, then buy yours at an optical store; safety glasses should be comfortable. Forget woodworking if you lose your sight. Very few sightless people run table saws, although Paul did have one student who was completely blind—and this particular man built a pair of speakers that rivaled everyone's in the class.

Don't wear jewelry—This includes watches, and take off those rings! You don't want to wear anything that can get caught in a machine. Bracelets, necklaces, rings, war medals—all jewelry should come off.

Don't wear loose clothing—If you are wearing long sleeves, roll them up above your elbows. You wouldn't believe how a running machine can reach out and grab clothing. I know certain people who wouldn't be caught dead without their baseball caps, but if that cap isn't glued to your head, don't wear it. And if you have long hair, like I do, get it up and out of the way. This doesn't mean braiding it down your back; a braid has a way of sneaking over your shoulder and getting in the way. Given a chance, a machine will scalp you.

Read your owner's manual for each machine—Then read each manual again. Get familiar with your equipment before running it. But what if you bought used and didn't get an instruction manual? In most cases, you can write the company for a manual. If the tool is obsolete, look in the back of woodworking magazines for someone selling the same thing, or advertise yourself. Pay particular attention to the "Don't do this" part of the manual. Paul and I will cover safety as we go along, just to refresh your memory.

Unplug your machine before working on it—This is an important habit to develop. If you are changing a blade, unplug the saw. If you are changing a router bit, unplug the router. Even if you are changing a sanding belt on the sander, unplug the sander. Don't for one moment think that this is too much trouble to go to. If you get lazy, you get hurt!

Don't run machinery if you are tired or distracted in any way—Alcohol and machines don't mix. Drugs and machines don't mix. If you are tired, hungry, angry, or if someone is just standing around talking to you, don't run your machines. I know some people who put TVs in their shop, which in my mind is tantamount to begging for an accident. Granted, finishing work can get tedious; background music from a radio can break the monotony, but I still don't recommend it, since you might be tempted to leave that radio there and turn it on when you are working with machines. The thing to remember is, if you aren't focused on your work, you risk injury.

Keep the shop clean—A clean workshop is a safe workshop. Not only do you create a fire hazard by leaving piles of sawdust lying around, but if you work on a concrete floor, the sawdust will turn it into a skating rink. The last thing you need is to slip while running a machine.

Keep your tools picked up. If you don't, you'll waste a lot of time trying to find them. I usually drag out the tools I need and then at the end of the day put everything away.

Keep safety equipment handy—Hang a first-aid kit on a wall, so it's readily available. I'm not talking about repairing serious injuries here: Just include the basics to patch up minor scrapes (blood is hard to sand out of light woods), and a pair of tweezers for splinters.

A fire extinguisher is essential—hang it next to your safety kit, within easy reach. Make sure you know how to use your fire extinguisher. In case of an emergency, you won't have time to read the instructions.

Since I often work alone, I usually take a portable phone into the shop with me. It's smart to have one nearby in case an accident happens. Tape a list of emergency numbers right to the handset.

Table-saw safety

PAM: If you get into the habit of paying attention to your work, then you increase the likelihood that you will be able to react if something goes wrong. However, when it comes to kickback, which happens in the blink of an eye, there is no time to react. I heard a lot about kickback before I started woodworking. Just

Aligning the table saw: At the base of the blade, measure the distance between the way and the marked sawtooth.

about every woodworker I knew told me to beware. I was ready to approach my saw with a helmet, full face-mask, and a flack jacket.

PAUL: When I met Pam, practically the first word out of her mouth was "kickback." She was very concerned about this shop hazard, as any woodworker should be. Kickback is just that, the wood is kicked out of the saw and thrown back, toward you, at an amazing velocity. It's caused by the wood getting pinched between the blade and the fence, and can cause serious injuries.

Kickback can easily be avoided if you follow a few simple rules, maintain your saw properly, and understand the process of milling wood. Here is some information to help you do just that.

The ways—Before you start work with any tool you have just purchased, check to see if everything is accurately aligned. In the case of the table saw, the first thing that must be done is to make sure the blade is parallel to the ways (the ways are the miter-gauge slots). If the saw-

Rotate the blade downward, then measure the distance between the way and the marked tooth.

blade is not parallel to the ways, it's very difficult to make square cuts, and the blade can catch the wood, bind it, and cause kickback.

Here's how to check. With the sawblade in place, and the machine unplugged, mark a tooth on the blade with a pencil, crayon, or magic marker. Rotate the blade so the marked tooth just comes up through the back of the throat plate. Measure the distance between the tooth and the way. Rotate the blade forward until the tooth is just starting to go down through the front of the throat plate and measure this distance. If the distances are not equal, you have to adjust the table. Loosen the bolts that anchor the table to the stand or motor mounts; continue rotating the blade to the back and then the front until the blade tooth measures an equal distance. Then tighten the bolts.

The Fence—Once the blade is aligned with the ways, adjust the fence to give a proper cut and reduce the chance of kickback. Adjust the fence parallel to the blade the same way you adjusted the blade to the ways—use the same marked tooth and rotate the blade. Note, however, that in the back, the fence should toe out, away from the blade. To do this, place an open matchbook cover (or something of similar thickness) next to the tooth as it comes up at the rear. This small difference will not appreciably effect the parallel rip cut of a board, but it will keep the back of the blade from lifting the board up and throwing it out of the saw. After your adjustments, rip a small board and observe the kerf marks as shown in the drawing; readjust as necessary.

Always use the correct blade to make the desired cut. Don't use a crosscut blade when ripping, or a rip blade when crosscutting. Keep sawblades sharp and clean—a dull blade, or a blade that is loaded with pitch, acts like a paddle in water, creating resistance and slapping rather than cutting.

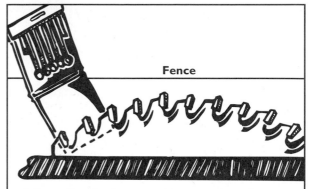

Adjust the rip fence so it toes minutely away from the blade. If the teeth at the front of the blade touch the fence, the space at the back should be the thickness of a matchbook cover.

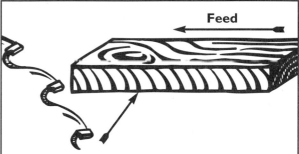

These marks indicate the front of the blade is cutting and the fence adjustment is fine.

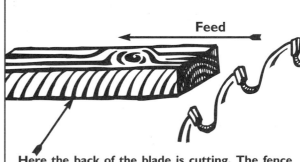

Here the back of the blade is cutting. The fence toes in toward the blade.

Blade and fence are parallel. Readjust the fence so the blade toes away from the blade.

Blade height—Adjust your blade so that it protrudes no more than one tooth (or $1/4$ in.) above the wood. On construction sites you'll see the sawblade raised as high as it can go. You'll also notice that more than a few construction workers are missing their fingers. On the other hand, if your blade is too low, the wood can crawl up on top of the sawblade and kickback will occur. Adjusting the blade height is easy; lay the wood next to the blade and raise or lower the blade accordingly.

Infeed and outfeed tables—Also known as extension tables, these are tables that you build or buy, which are the same height as the table saw and can be placed where needed to support long boards while being crosscut or ripped. Forget trying to balance a board while running it through the saw. Fighting the weight of a board that is cantilevering off the table will put you out of control, and leave you open to serious injuries.

As we discussed in Chapter 1, if you opt not to use the factory guard that comes with your table saw, you should substitute anti-kick -back wheels. These wheels attach to the fence and hold the board down and against the fence at the same time. Also, the wheels on my saw turn only in one direction—forward—thereby preventing the board from backing up and kicking out of the saw.

Pushsticks—You never want your fingers close to the blade while it is running, so pushblocks and/or pushsticks are essential devices. These handy tools come in a variety of shapes and sizes. You can buy a bunch of them and figure out which suits you the best. Or you can build your own (Chapter 6). Either way, get some and use them. Even if you have anti-kickback wheels on your saw, use a pushstick to finish the cut.

Crosscutting—Thankfully, crosscutting (cutting across the grain) is easy. Use your miter gauge and stand to the side of the sawblade. Leave the free end of the wood alone— if you try to push the free end through the blade along with the other piece, the wood could bind in the saw, which will cause kickback. Once the cut has been made, wait for the blade to come to a complete stop before pulling away the cutoff. And stay away from the cutoff while the saw is coming to a stop, because you never know when the teeth might grab the cutoff and send it flying.

When you are crosscutting long boards, use a miter gauge extension for support (Chapter 6). I suggest maple, which is sturdy. If the blade guard will not allow the extension to be pushed clear of the saw after the cut, don't pull the extension back toward you while the saw is running; shut off the saw and then reposition the miter extension. Never try to back anything out of a running blade. Always push the wood forward. If you can't push the wood forward for some reason, say it's binding or it's stuck on something, shut off the saw. It you try to back it out, you will eat it, thanks to kickback.

Don't crosscut a board using the fence as a stop to make multiple cuts of the same length. These pieces will always twist or turn between the blade and fence, and will get kicked out of the saw. A spacer block at least $3/4$ in. thick should always be used to avoid this hazard.

Don't stand directly behind the sawblade.

When using the fence as a stop for crosscutting, clamp a $3/4$-in. thick spacer to the fence.

A miter-gauge extension supports long boards during crosscutting.

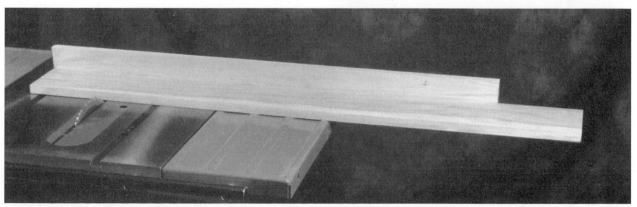

Infeed and outfeed extension tables support long boards before and after a ripping cut.

Here's the correct in-feed position for a right-handed person when ripping wood. Always use both hands—your right hand supports and pushes the wood through the blade, while your left keeps the wood snug against the fence.

Ripping—In ripping, the fence supports and guides the wood while a cut is made along the grain. If the board is long, you need to support the wood on infeed and outfeed tables (Chapter 6). Stand to the left side of the blade if the fence is on the right; never stand directly behind the wood.

Use two hands when you are ripping, and always pay attention to where the wood is against the fence—you don't want the board wandering around. The sawblade isn't going anywhere but the board sure can, and if it wanders, you're going to have problems. Finish the cut with a pushstick or pushblock. If you didn't start the cut with either of these tools, then you'll have to pick one up to finish. That's fine, but don't let go of the wood with your other hand. Once your pushblock is in place, remove your left hand and finish with the pushblock.

When ripping thin wood, substitute a featherboard for your left hand to hold the stock snug against the fence. Finish the cut with a very thin pushstick.

I don't suggest any beginner try to rip large pieces of plywood or other sheet material. Use your jigsaw or hand crosscut saw to break down large sheets into manageable sizes.

A few more table saw rules—Never try to freehand anything through the saw—ever. If you've

got a weird cut and you can't figure out a way to support the wood with a fence or miter gauge, then get out your jigsaw or handsaw.

Always use pushsticks and featherboards for any cut that you deem to be even remotely dangerous. Never try to force a board through the blade. Conversely, don't use a light touch either, because the board can back up and be thrown out of the saw. I guess the best advice is to use a gentle, but persuasive, touch. This comes with experience. If you are unsure of a cut, unplug the saw and walk through it until you are comfortable with the procedure.

Never rip or crosscut a warped or twisted board. The board will not lie flat on the table. It will crawl on top of the blade and can be ejected in any direction, backward or sideways.

Never leave the blade exposed. When you are done using your saw for the day, retract the sawblade below the surface of the table. This protects your blade and you.

Most importantly, think before you saw!

Router safety

PAM: While a router is less intimidating than a table saw, it can be dangerous nonetheless. Again, observe the basic shop safety rules discussed at the beginning of this chapter. Since a router spews out plenty of sawdust, you'll need to wear a dust mask if you don't have a dust-collection system.

Make sure there are no burrs on the router-bit shank. Burrs can damage the collet (the jaws that hold the router bit), and will keep the bit from being securely tightened; if you can't tighten the bit all the way, then it can edge down as the router is running, ruining your cut. Very small burrs can be removed by gently hand-sanding with wet and dry silicon carbide paper; if the burrs are large, discard the bit.

Always insert the bit shank all the way into the collet, but make sure the fillet, where the shank and the cutter body meet, is not

Use the miter slot to position the featherboard, or clamp it to the table, almost (but not quite) aligned with the sawteeth—if your featherboard overlaps the sawblade, it will bind the wood and cause kickback.

clamped in the collet. On most bits this isn't a problem, yet if you tighten the collet on the fillet, which is actually bigger than the shaft itself, than you really haven't tightened the bit, and the bit can drop out while routing, creating a potential for injury. Also, this can permanently enlarge the collet—called a "sprung collet," which will render the collet useless. Periodically check the bit after tightening to see if there is any slippage. If there is, the collet is sprung and must be thrown away.

Hold the router comfortably at arms'

As you finish a ripping cut, use a pushstick or pushblock to help you clear the blade.

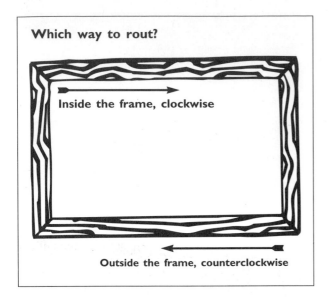

Which way to rout?

Inside the frame, clockwise

Outside the frame, counterclockwise

length, neither so close to your body that it can grab your clothes, nor so far away that your overextended arms have little control. Never over-reach a cut, because you can lose your balance and hurt yourself.

Make sure you have enough cord to make the cut. If you have to adjust the cord while cutting, your attention will be diverted from the router.

A router bit turns clockwise when hand-held, and counter clockwise when inverted, as in a router table. Whatever position your router is in, always feed the work against the rotation. I know this can be confusing at first. When the router is in the router table, you always go the same way, from right to left. If the router is hand-held, look at the diagram and figure out what you are doing. Most of the time you will be routing from left to right, but there are times you won't be. If you feed the work with the rotation of the bit, the router will want to skip and pull away from the board. If this happens, stop and figure out why. Are you going the wrong way? Is something wrong with the bit? Correct the problem before continuing.

Never try to make a deep cut all at once. Not only will the bit burn the wood, but you will lose control of the router. Instead, make

several shallow passes at the work, cutting deeper with every pass.

If you can't get a bit out of the router, and this happens a lot, don't grab the pliers and start yanking on it. Instead, give the collet nut a sharp rap with one of the router wrenches (don't hit the bit), and the bit will come out.

Whenever possible, rout with the grain of the wood, because this will cause less tear-out. If you have to rout against the grain, make very shallow cuts. Yes, it will take longer, but it's the only way to avoid tear-out. Also, use shallow cuts when routing through knots.

I will discuss router table safety when we build the router table (Chapter 8). If you already have a router table, then look ahead to that chapter and read up on safety.

PAUL: When using a tool for the first time, be it a table saw, router, or jigsaw, I have found it helpful to read the safety instructions both before and after tool usage. Read critically, thinking back to moves you made that could possibly have caused injury. Then avoid that action in the future. There are so many things for a beginner to think about that it's not uncommon to overlook a few safety requirements, but you don't want to make a habit of it. Likewise, it's a good idea to periodically review the safety information in your owner's manual after you have been using a tool for a while. This way you can verify that you're doing everything correctly, and change the way you handle things if you're not.

14 SAFETY POINTS

1. Think before you proceed. Don't work in the shop if you are tired or distracted.

2. Wear safety glasses at all times.

3. Wear short-sleeved clothing, or roll long sleeves up past your elbows.

4. Take off that jewelry.

5. Pull long hair up and out of the way.

6. Regularly police work surfaces to keep them clean and uncluttered.

7. Keep all tools unplugged when not in use.

8. Know the tool before using it (read tool safety instructions).

9. Keep all guards in place and functioning properly.

10. Keep cutters sharp; inspect them regularly for damage.

11. Keep all cutters properly tightened; make sure they rotate easily.

12. Store pushsticks and pushblocks within easy reach.

13. Adjust hold-downs and featherboards to proper tension.

14. Make sure you are comfortable with a cut before making the actual cut (read your owner's manual if you're unsure of a procedure).

ELECTRICAL SAFETY

CAUSE

1. Check all tool cords. If they are frayed or damaged, repair or discard.

2. Make sure grounding prongs on tools and extension cords are not loose, damaged, or missing.

3. Make sure all surfaces are dry and there is no standing or open containers of water (includes glasses and cups) in close vicinity of electrical tools or outlets.

4. Use the proper wire gauge to conduct the most current for the length of extension cord.

5. Make sure switches don't arc (spark.) Turn power off at service or sub-panel. Remove switch plate and blow out dust.

EFFECT

1. Possible electrical shock.

2. Possible electrical shock.

3. Shock to maximum shock (death).

4. If wire gauge is too small, motors will not run at optimum performance, creating possible electrical overload, fire, or physical injury (to the motor or to you).

5. Possible fire.

5 THE LUMBERYARD MAZE

Types of Lumber

PAUL: Wood is available as either softwood or hardwood, but since there is extremely hard softwood and very soft hardwood, the names don't necessarily accurately describe all the woods within each grouping. Instead, the term softwood refers to wood produced by any conifer or evergreen tree. These trees have needle-shaped leaves that are retained by the tree year-round, and the seeds are open (as in a pinecone), not encased by a shell. By contrast, hardwoods are produced by deciduous trees, which shed their leaves annually; the seeds are either enclosed by a hard shell (walnuts, pecans, acorns) or by a pulpy mass (cherries, apples, lemons). The main difference between hardwoods and softwoods is in the composition of the cell structure, and the amount of resin (sap in softwoods, gum in hardwoods), they contain. Resin inhibits staining and gluing, and can build up on your machines. Softwoods contain a large amount of resin.

Softwoods

PAUL: Most pine that is purchased at a lumberyard or home center is kiln-dried (a process described later in this chapter) initially, but left outside in the weather. It doesn't much matter, since this wood is meant to be used for home-building and is held in position by nails until completely dry. Dimensional pine is smooth on all surfaces and the edges are slightly rounded. The projects in this book are mostly of pine, since it's inexpensive compared to hardwoods (and therefore less costly to replace when you mess up).

There are some softwoods that are used exclusively for furniture building: Idaho white pine and sugar pine are used for furniture; Tennessee red cedar for blanket and cedar chests; and English yew for small boxes. These softwoods are usually available only at the hardwood lumberyard—they're milled and marketed using special grades and come in random lengths and widths. They have very little resin and have been kiln-dried to make them easier to machine and finish.

Pine measurement—Pine boards come in standard dimensions such as 1x2, 2x4, and 4x4. The first number designates thickness, the second width. These are called nominal dimensions. The actual dimensions are somewhat smaller. The thickness of a 2x4, for example, is 1-1/2 in., while the width is 3-1/2 in. Why is this? Well, very simply, the mill dresses all surfaces before shipping—both faces of each board are planed, and both edges are jointed smooth, and there goes the thickness and width. You have to get used to reading dimensional pine by its actual dimensions, not what the bin label says. For reference when planning a project, refer to the dimensional lumber chart.

Softwood grades—The grade of a board is determined by the number of defects or knots in the wood. Here are the common grades:

No. 1 common: This is perfectly clear wood, with no defects. Since so little of this wood is available on the market, No. 1 and No. 2 common are combined in the lumber bins.

No. 2 common: This lumber may have knots up to 2-1/2 in. (in narrow boards) and 3-1/2-in. (in wider boards). The knots must be "tight," that is, coming from a limb that was growing as part of the

DIMENSIONAL LUMBER CHART

Nominal size	Actual dimensions
1x2	3/4" x 1-1/2"
1x4	3/4" x 3-1/2"
1x6	3/4" x 5-1/2"
1x8	3/4" x 7-1/4"
1x10	3/4" x 9-1/4"
1x12	3/4" x 11-1/4"
2x2	1-1/2" x 1-1/2"
2x4	1-1/2" x 3-1/2"
2x6	1-1/2" x 5-1/2"
2x8	1-1/2" x 7-1/4"
2x10	1-1/2" x 9-1/4"
2x12	1-1/2" x 11-1/4"
4x4	3-1/2" x 3-1/2"

All softwood lumber is sold in two-foot length multiples, that is 8 ft., 10 ft., 12 ft., etc.

Stickering Lumber

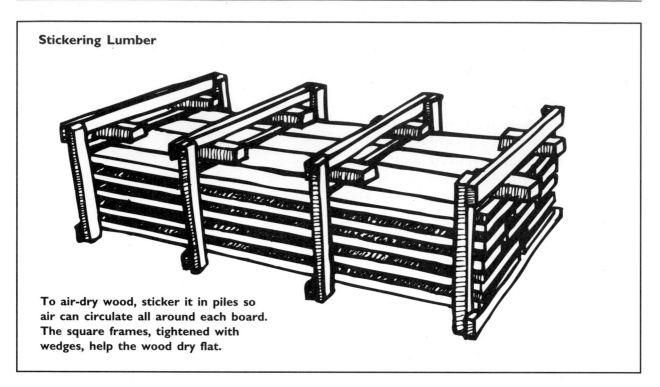

To air-dry wood, sticker it in piles so air can circulate all around each board. The square frames, tightened with wedges, help the wood dry flat.

tree. (A "loose" knot occurs when the tree trunk grew around the limb.)

No. 3 common: This lumber may have all the defects found in No. 2 common, plus loose knots and knotholes. No. 3 common can be used for small projects if you cut the clear wood out from between the knots.

Air- and kiln-drying—Moisture may be removed from wood by either air- or kiln-drying. The advantage of air-drying is low cost; disadvantages are the long drying period, and the relatively high moisture content (rarely below 16 percent) of the "dry" wood.

Wood to be air-dried is stacked and stickered in piles so that each board receives adequate ventilation. This arrangement hastens drying and equalizes moisture loss—if more moisture is lost from one surface than another, the wood will warp. Obviously, the speed with which the wood will dry depends on the weather. Cold, damp weather will slow down the process; hot, dry weather will speed it up to the point where the wood is damaged from losing moisture too quickly. Warm, humid climates can promote the growth of fungi that will stain and decay wood.

Kiln-dried lumber is dried in a kiln, a large, sealed chamber that regulates temperature, humidity, and air movement. The temperature in the chamber is raised to 110 to 180 degrees for hardwoods, and up to 220 degrees for softwood. The moisture content of the wood is regularly monitored—when it drops to between 6 and 8 percent, the wood is considered dry and removed from the kiln.

Hardwoods

PAUL: Even though your main concern right now is softwood, you will eventually be using hardwood, since that is what most furniture is made from. Accordingly, there is a lot to learn about the grading and purchase of hardwood lumber.

Hardwoods are milled, dried, and marketed differently from softwoods. Because hardwood is expensive, it's desirable to use as much of the tree as possible. When a hardwood log is sawn, the resulting board is wider at one end, tapering from the bottom to the top. Since hardwoods are so valuable, the edges of the board are not sawn parallel as is done with softwoods. The same is true with length—softwoods are crosscut to even lengths; hardwoods are the length the log will yield. Hardwood lumber is therefore sold in pieces of random width and length.

Measuring hardwoods—The thickness of a hardwood board is measured in quarters of an inch: 4/4 (four quarters) equals 1 in., 5/4 (five quarters) equals 1-¼ in., 6/4 (six quarters) equals 1-½ in., and so on. Hardwoods are usually sold in the rough on both faces and edges. Some retailers, realizing that not all their customers have planers, plane the boards on both

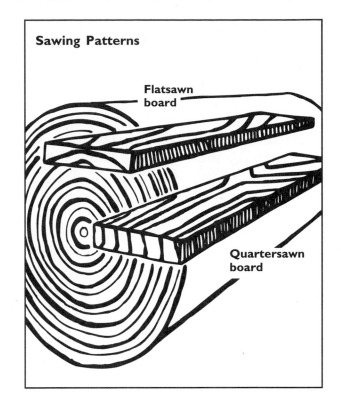

Sawing Patterns

Flatsawn board

Quartersawn board

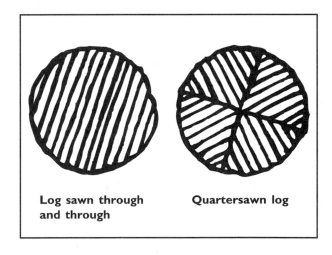

Log sawn through and through

Quartersawn log

faces and will even straight-line-rip them on one edge for those who don't have jointers. (It's important to note that you pay for the full thickness of the wood, even though some has been lost to planing and ripping.)

It's usually most economical to buy your wood at a hardwood retailer. Though some larger home centers sell 4/4 hardwood in widths of 4, 6, and 8 in., in lengths of 4 to 8 ft., this is an expensive way to buy lumber.

The board foot—Since hardwoods are sold in random widths and lengths, they are measured by the board foot, which takes into account the thickness, width, and length of any given board. A board foot is a measure of volume equivalent to a square foot that is one inch thick. How do you determine the amount of lumber to buy? Follow this formula to figure board feet: thickness in inches(T) times width in inches(W) times length in inches (L) divided by 144 (number of inches in one square foot). However, if you are figuring length in feet, not inches, then the divisor is 12: 12 in. wide x 1 ft. long = 12 running-inches-per-foot. You must pay attention to which form of measurement you are using for length—inches or feet.

Length in inches	Length in feet
$\dfrac{T'' \times W'' \times L''}{144} = BDFT$	$\dfrac{T'' \times W'' \times L'}{12} = BDFT$

Here's an example: You have a board that is 1 in. thick, 6 in. wide, and 96 in. long. The formula looks like this:

$$\frac{1'' \times 6'' \times 96''}{144} = 4 \text{ BDFT}$$

Take the same board, with the length measured in feet, and the formula looks like this:

$$\frac{1'' \times 6'' \times 8'}{12} = 4 \text{ BDFT}$$

In all the years I have been teaching woodworking, the concept of calculating board feet

has been one of the most difficult to get across. So I came up with a couple of ways of making board feet easier to figure. The first is to eliminate division.

$$\text{Length in inches} = \frac{1}{144}'' = .006944$$

and

$$\text{Length in feet} = \frac{1}{144} = .0833$$

So the formula would be:

Length in inches	Length in feet
$T'' \times W'' \times L'' \times .006944$	$T'' \times W'' \times L' \times .0833$

Using the same board as in previous examples,

$1'' \times 6'' \times 96'' \times .006944 = 3.999 \text{ BDFT}$
$1'' \times 6'' \times 8' \times .0833 = 3.998 \text{ BDFT}$

As you see, both calculations come close to 4 BDFT, certainly close enough to estimate the amount and cost of wood required for a project.

In the examples, I have used only 4/4 (1-in. thick) lumber. This is because hardwoods thinner than 1 in. are converted into board feet just as though they were 4/4 stock. Thicknesses greater than 4/4 are figured more accurately; a 5/4 board (1-1/4 in. thick) is considered 1-1/4 in., not 2 in., thick. To figure board footage using thicker wood, I turn the fractions into decimals because it's much easier to multiply. One quarter = .25, so if you have a 5/4 board it's 4/4 + 1/4, or 1.25. Here are some other common thicknesses:

5/4 = 1.25"	8/4 = 2"	12/4 = 3"
6/4 = 1.5"	10/4 = 2.5"	16/4 = 4"

Particleboard, fiberboard, and plywood

PAUL: Most beginning woodworkers avoid the use of particleboard and fiberboard because of the misconception that they aren't as "real" as real wood. I argue that these fabricated products add structural stability, save expense and time, and, most importantly, save trees by allowing valuable hardwoods to be used more judiciously. Most accomplished cabinetmakers use particleboard, and fiberboard wherever it is appropriate, and you should, too.

Particleboard—Particleboard was developed in Europe after World War II because the forests had been destroyed and there was very little usable standing lumber. It was formulated by using waste wood from sawmills and other wood manufacturing processes. In the early 1950s, particleboard was being produced in the United States; by the late 1960s, the particleboard industry was the fastest growing industry in wood manufacturing.

Particleboard comes in two grades: construction and furniture (high-density). Construction-grade particleboard has coarse wood flakes on the surface, and, as its name decrees, is used in construction. It is available in 4'x8' sheets.

Furniture-grade (high-density) particleboard has finer flakes, resulting in a smooth surface that is excellent for veneering. It comes in 49-in. by 97-in. panels (this peculiar width and length allows for saw kerfs in cabinet manufacturing; a saw kerf is the wood that has been removed by the sawblade during a cut.) You may have to special-order furniture-grade particleboard from your wood supplier, since the majority goes to furniture manufacturers and to specialty lumber dealers.

Particleboard has many desirable properties when used in furnituremaking: low cost, smoothness, and stability—and it won't split or splinter. Its drawback is its heaviness, and you have to work it with power tools. While particleboard can be cut with a handsaw, it's hard work and the material will rapidly dull the tool.

Fiberboard—Fiberboard is a lot like particleboard, but it holds fasteners better, can be veneered, is more stable, and stays smooth even if there is a change in humidity. It is produced from the same material as particleboard (wood flakes made from sawmill waste). The amount of pressure used to form the final board determines the grade of the product. The one you're most interested in is medium-density fiberboard. This material is superior to particleboard for building furniture and cabinets—you can use it for any part that will be painted or veneered. (It cannot be used where heavy loads will be applied, such as aprons, backs, or chair legs, unless several layers of fiberboard have been laminated together.) It is also excellent for making patterns to duplicate parts.

Plywood—With the exception of hardwood plywood (hardwood veneer is glued onto either side of a lumber core), and Baltic birch plywood (all plies are made from birch), plywood isn't used in fine furniture construction, or even when making shop furniture. Construction ply (although full of knots) has the advantage of not weighing as much as other sheet materials, but its one big disadvantage is that the face veneer shreds, resulting in many splinters under the fingernails—no plywood was ever meant to have anything dragged over its surface. Construction grades are meant to be covered up with carpeting, drywall, or insulation.

How to buy lumber

PAM: Take your time when purchasing lumber. Thoroughly check the wood for defects such as knots, checks, or splits. Knots aren't necessarily bad—if they're red or brown, they are known as tight knots and are an integral part of the wood. But if a knot has a black ring around it, and is separated from the surrounding wood by bark, dirt, or fungus, then it's a loose knot. It will fall out while working the wood or after the project is finished.

Checks are splits in the wood that can occur during kiln-drying, while the wood is being transported, or in the lumberyard. A few

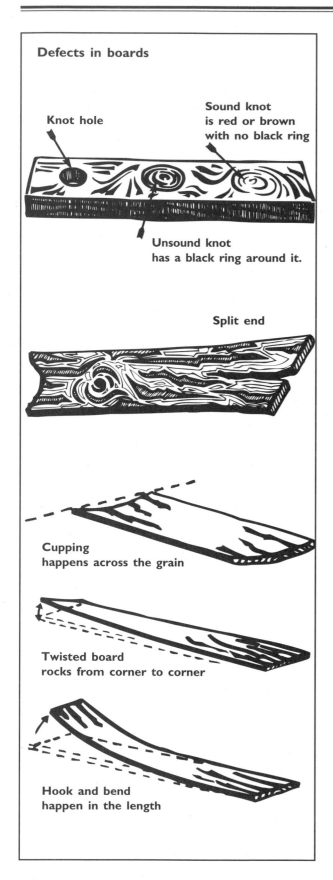

Defects in boards

Knot hole

Sound knot
is red or brown
with no black ring

Unsound knot
has a black ring around it.

Split end

Cupping
happens across the grain

Twisted board
rocks from corner to corner

Hook and bend
happen in the length

minor checks on the ends of a board are permissible, even to be expected—they normally happen in the drying process, and can easily be trimmed off. Wide checks in the middle of the board that don't reach either surface indicate that the board was improperly dried—the checks could penetrate the entire interior of the board, a condition called honeycomb. When the board is planed or sawn, the honeycomb checks are exposed, and it really does look like a honeycomb. A honeycombed board is worthless in structure and appearance.

Splits are large cracks that start at the end of a board and progress down its length for a considerable distance. Machining a split board is risky because the wood may split the rest of the way, which will either bind the blade or cause the wood to fly out of the machine. Never buy split wood.

Also make sure that the wood isn't cupped, bowed, or twisted. A board is cupped if it curves across the grain. Sometimes these boards can be ripped into very narrow widths and used as cleats, glue blocks, story poles, or frame stock. A bowed board curves along the grain. This type of board can sometimes be crosscut into shorter lengths and used in small projects where the board is restricted from moving, such as in blocking and bracing, or in shelves in a small cabinet. Twisted lumber will rock from corner to diagonal corner when laid on a flat surface. The board is literally twisted. (This condition is also known as wind, pronounced to rhyme with rind). Twisted lumber is suitable only for use as small pieces of blocking and bracing.

You should always shoot for purchasing straight lumber—it's just easier for beginners to work on. At the lumberyard, if you have to dig through an entire stack of lumber to find straight boards, then do so. Salespeople usually don't mind you going through the lumber as long as you restack it the way you found it.

Storing lumber

PAM: If you have purchased dimensional pine, put it in your shop (providing your shop is in the house, and warm) and let it acclimate for about a month. This gives the wood a chance to dry out, and if the lumber is going to warp, twist, or check, it will usually do so within this period. If you acclimate the wood, you won't have any nasty surprises when you start building. However, most people don't plan this far ahead, and they pay for it later when the wood warps and splits, ruining the piece.

Don't store lumber by standing it on end and leaning it against the wall. This will induce a bow in the boards that usually can't be reversed. Also, don't lay boards on a concrete floor because the wood will draw moisture out of the concrete and the boards will warp. Instead, store lumber at least 12 in. above a concrete floor; if you have to set the lumber on concrete, lay down a sheet of plastic for a vapor barrier first. Always allow any lumber to acclimate to the temperature and humidity of your shop before using it.

There is no guarantee that once you get your wood home it won't warp. The merchant cannot be held responsible for what happens to a board once it leaves the yard. However, if you crosscut more than a few inches up from the end and find it has checks throughout its interior, take it back; a reputable merchant will replace the board or refund your money.

That should get you started. Know what you're looking for, know what you're buying, and use what you buy. Plan judiciously. Lumber isn't cheap; it's a commodity that will continue to rise in price as the world's forests are depleted. Paul has lumber in his collection that will never again be available on the market —the trees are extinct. As you are building projects, keep your scrap, which later can be used for all sorts of purposes. When you finally do fill up a box of tiny unusable pieces, check with your woodworking guild or a woodworker's store to see where you can recycle them.

6 TABLE-SAW ACCESSORIES

PAM: Don't let the word "accessories" fool you—these shop tools are necessities, essential for safe woodworking. In this chapter, you will build a miter-gauge extension, to safely support long lengths of wood through a crosscut; extension tables, also to support wood; and pushsticks and pushblocks, to help get wood safely past the blade. Let's look at each one.

You absolutely need extension tables for your table saw; otherwise, how will you support long boards? Forget about strength. The strength of Tarzan won't help you here. You can't infeed wood and outfeed it at the same time—nobody can be in two places at once. And extension tables, when not in use supporting wood, come in handy as auxiliary workbenches.

Extension tables are easy to build: a top, an apron, and four legs. Make a big one and a small one—you don't need two large tables. I use the small table for infeed since I'm also standing there supporting the wood; the big extension table catches all the wood as it comes off the saw table.

Making a few extension tables is a great way to practice your gluing technique; if you slop the glue all over the place, it won't matter, since it'll be underneath the table.

A miter-gauge extension, used for crosscutting long boards, is a long, straight board that supports the wood as it's being fed through the blade. If you don't use support, long boards tend to go cockeyed, resulting in a diagonal cut instead of a straight one. And if the wood tilts,

Use a miter-gauge extension—a straight, long board screwed to the table saw's miter gauge— to support long boards during crosscutting.

and binds in the blade, you could be in for some nasty kickback. It's much safer to use a miter-gauge extension.

Pushsticks and pushblocks are simple to produce. Shop-built ones are usually superior to commercial products, because you can customize them as necessary. And, if you run one of your pushsticks through the blade, it's no big deal—just make a new one.

Before you begin to build....

PAUL: You'll need some hardware and tools to make the projects in this chapter. Buy whatever you don't have on hand. You'll see I recommend using leg levelers—if your floor is perfectly flat, and you have confidence that you can cut the leg height exactly, you can forget them. On the other hand, if you don't use levelers and find you have slight deviations in the floor, you will be forever shimming the table.

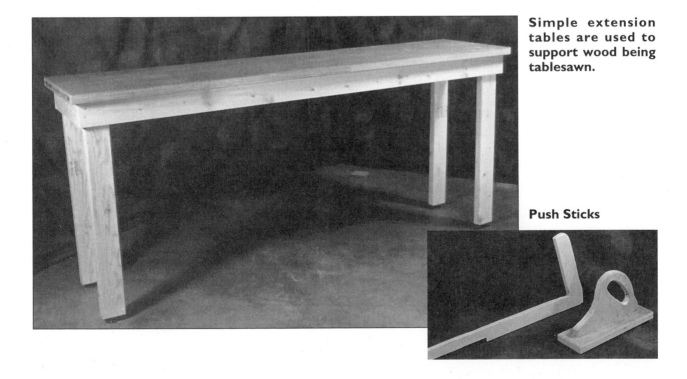

Simple extension tables are used to support wood being tablesawn.

Push Sticks

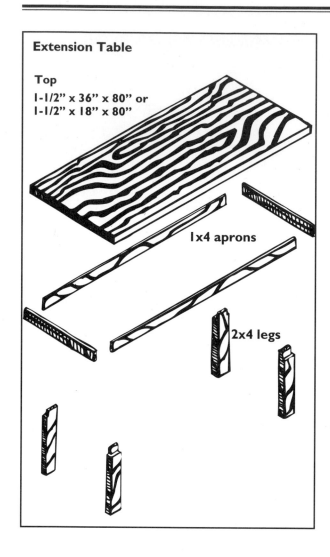

Extension Table

Top
1-1/2" x 36" x 80" or
1-1/2" x 18" x 80"

1x4 aprons

2x4 legs

You need the following items:

- Drywall or wood screws (1¼ in. long)
- Drill and bits
- Leg levelers and tee-nuts
- Yellow wood glue or polyurethane wood glue (see section on gluing later in this chapter)
- 12-in. or 18-in. bar clamps (at least 6)
- 36-in. pipe clamps (1 or 2)
- Sawhorses (2)
- Combination square
- Jigsaw
- Jigsaw blades for cutting tight radiuses (pushstick handles). Look on the blade package, it should tell you what the blade is meant for; otherwise, a 6 or 10 tpi (teeth per inch) blade.

How much wood do you need?

PAUL: Dimensions here are relative. You can make the extension tables as big or small as you want. Your shop might not accommodate the large extension tables I built; Pam's shop barely does. So, how big is your shop? We will come back to this in a minute, but right now you need to decide on what you are going to use for the table tops, since this impacts table dimensions. Create a lumber list for each extension table as you read through the sections describing the various parts. Then put the two lists together to see how much wood you need to buy.

Materials for the table top—Hollow-core doors make fine tops for extension tables. This isn't a dining room table, so don't even think about hardwoods. For Pam's tables, we used damaged, hollow-core doors which I picked up cheap at a home center. If you go with doors, make sure you get ones with smooth, untextured, surfaces. And don't buy solid-core doors. Extension tables must be portable, and solid-core doors make them too heavy.

A disadvantage of hollow-core doors is that you are stuck with standard dimensions—you can't cut a hollow-core door down to size, because if you whack off an end, you'll ruin the structural integrity of the door and it will eventually collapse upon itself. For Pam's extension tables, we used one standard-size door (1³/₈ in. x 36 in. x 80 in.), and one narrow door (measuring 18 in. wide). Two standard-size doors wouldn't have fit into her shop.

If you don't like the idea of hollow-core doors, you can go with particleboard. (Don't use fir plywood, because it shreds.) Although a particleboard top will make the table heavier to drag around, you can size the tops to fit your shop. In many cases, lumberyards will cut the particleboard to size for a reasonable fee.

So what will it be, hollow-core doors or particleboard? Whatever you use, you need to figure out the table top dimensions now, before you can figure out how much lumber you will need for the apron and legs.

Material for the table legs—Make the table legs from 2x4 pine. (If you botch a piece, it won't kill you to replace it.) Refer to Chapter 5 and read about dimensional lumber.

Roughly figure the leg height by measuring from the floor to about 3 in. above the table saw surface (give yourself some extra wood).

Here's an example: Suppose the legs are 31-in. long 2x4s and you need four of them. Multiplying 31 in. by 4 legs results in 124 in. Since dimensional lumber isn't sold in inches, divide the total by 12, to yield 10.33 feet. When you consult the dimensional lumber chart in Chapter 5, you'll see that a 10-ft. long 2x4 won't give enough lumber, but a 12-ft. length would. If you don't want to haul a 12-ft.

long board, you can buy two 8-ft. boards instead, and plan on having some scrap.

Material for the table apron—An apron is used as a brace to keep the top flat; it also gives the legs something to attach to. The apron is inset from the edges of the table top (so you have room to clamp things later on), but for now, treat the apron ends and sides as though they were the same length as the table ends and sides. Use 1x4 pine for all apron pieces.

More lumber—Also figure into your bill of material one or two straight 1x4x8s for the miter-gauge extension and one or two 1x2x8s for story poles.

You will also need a 1x2x8 for each indexing stick you make, usually three sticks if you're using a door for your table top, and one if you'll have a particleboard top. (They must be longer than the table top: Depending on the length of your table, you may need wood longer than 8 ft.) You use indexing sticks to brace the apron lengths (and other pieces) when you glue them; if you don't, you might end up with the apron going at angles you never imagined.

If you are using hollow-core doors, one indexing stick goes underneath the top, and the other one is used as a clamp block. If you don't use something as a clamp block, you will go right through the thin veneer covering the door when you tighten the clamps.

Getting down to work—Before you can build the extension tables, you need to make the miter-gauge extension to crosscut the legs and apron lengths, so let's do that first. Then we'll make the extension tables, and the pushsticks and pushblock. You will need all of these things to build the workbench in the next chapter.

Building the miter-gauge extension

PAM: It's up to you how long you want the extension, but make sure it's at least 6 in. longer than the length of your table legs, since you are going to clamp a stop block to the extension to make multiple leg cuts. You also want the extension to extend at least 12 in. past the sawblade on the other side, for balance. Once you fasten the extension to the miter gauge, you are going to make a cut through the extension, and this will give you a kerf (sawblade) reference. It's much easier to line up a cut with the kerf reference on the miter extension, than to try to position the wood and pencil mark against the sawblade all the time.

1. Mount a combination blade or crosscut blade on the saw.

2. Clamp the extension to the miter gauge, so it can't shift. Look at your miter gauge— you will see two holes that have been drilled through the face of it; these holes are for attaching extensions. Put a pencil through the hole and make a mark on the extension board; if the holes are too small to accept a pencil, then use a nail to dent the wood so you will know where to drill the pilot holes. (You drill a pilot so that the thread of a screw can cut into the wood without crushing it like a nail does. A pilot hole will also keep the screw from wandering, especially around knots or in highly figured wood.)

You need to drill pilot holes with a drill bit that is the root diameter of your screw. Hold a drill bit right in front of the screw and look at it eye level. If you can't see any screw threads, the bit is too big. If you can see the root diameter of the screw, the bit is a little too small. However, if you can see just the screw threads past the bit, but not

When drilling pilot holes for wood screws, figure out what size bit to use by holding the bit in front of the screw. If you can see the threads but not the root, it's the right size.

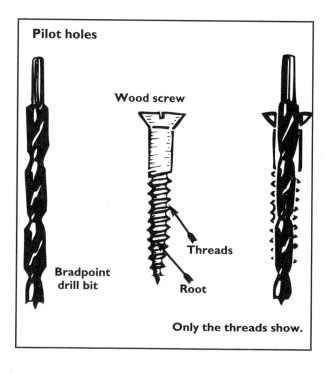

Pilot holes

Wood screw

Bradpoint drill bit

Threads

Root

Only the threads show.

the diameter (root) of the screw, the bit will work for pilot-hole drilling.

3. Unclamp the board from the miter gauge and clamp it to a sawhorse. Don't try and drill something that isn't clamped down— the bit can grab the board and send it spinning out of control; in the process you can lose control of the drill, sprain your wrist, or get hit by the board.

4. Drill the pilot holes through the board.

5. Set the extension board back on the saw and align the pilot holes with the miter gauge.

6. Screw the board into place on the miter gauge.

7. Adjust the sawblade to about 1 in. above the table.

8. With the miter-gauge extension attached to the miter gauge, crosscut the extension to create a kerf reference. You need only run the miter-gauge extension through the blade once. (If you don't cut a kerf reference now, you will when you use your miter-gauge extension the first time.)

Run the extension through the sawblade to create the kerf reference. This shows you where the saw will cut.

Making extension tables

PAM: Now that you have a miter-gauge extension, you're ready to build the extension tables. If you have opted for a particleboard top, don't even think of ripping it with your table saw without the help of extension tables. Instead, get out the sawhorses and use a jigsaw to cut the board to dimensions.

Constructing the apron

PAM: You don't want the apron flush with the edges of the table top. Later on you will need an edge for clamping things. With a particleboard top, inset the apron as far as a bar clamp will reach. But if you are using a hollow-core

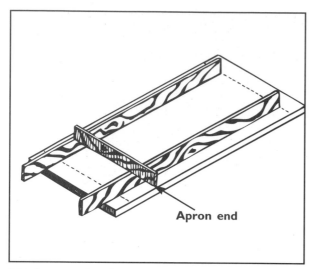

Mark apron lumber to length.

Use your combination square to position the apron with the edge of the extension table.

door top, you can't set the apron on the hollow-core part or you could drive the clamp right through the soft veneer. On a hollow-core door, there is only about 1-³/₈ in. of solid wood around the edges. Look at the bottom corner of the door and you can usually see where the solid wood ends and the hollow-core part begins. Place both apron sides and ends on the solid part of the door.

1. Place the apron side piece atop the table top and mark one side for length.

2. Set the board next to the table-saw blade, and adjust the blade one carbide tooth, but no more than ¹/₄ in., above the wood.

3. Crosscut the apron side to length. (Always cut the longest board first; if you cut it too short, you can still get shorter lengths, or in this case, ends, out of it.)

4. Transfer the apron length. Lay the cut apron side on top of the lumber for the second side, aligning the ends of the boards so they are even. Pencil-mark the second apron side to length. With this method you have to be sure to cut off the pencil line, but no more—it's one of the few times you will do so. The general rule is not to cut off the line. You are going to do this only with the really long boards, since it's hard to set a stop block on the miter gauge at this length.

5. Crosscut the second apron side to length.

6. Position the apron sides on the table top. Use your combination square to align them with the edges; you don't want the aprons veering off at angles to the edges. Set the handle of the combination square against the edge of the table, and push the rule forward to the length you want. Lock the square. Use the combination square up and down the length of the door to position the apron.

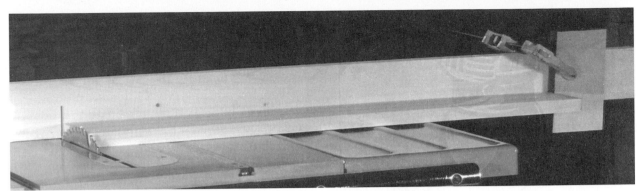

Set one apron end against the sawblade. At the other end, clamp a stop block (to the miter-gauge extension) against the end of the apron, to allow you to transfer the measurement to the second apron end.

Dry-clamp the apron into place, using three or four clamps, unless you're clamping a hollow-core door. In this case, clamp an indexing stick underneath the top so you won't go through the veneer. Use your combination square set to the apron depth to align the indexing stick. Clamp the indexing stick to the ends of the table, and then clamp the apron to the table. You can see this on p. 87.

7. Place the lumber for one apron end across the ends of the apron sides, as shown in the drawing. Mark the board to fit inside the apron sides.

8. Crosscut the apron end to length, but this time don't cut off the pencil line.

9. Set the apron end into place between the apron sides to check the fit. (If you've cut the end too long, trim it. If the end is too short, crosscut a new one.) Take the apron end back to the saw. Set the end of the apron against the sawblade (if you are using a carbide-tipped blade, make sure you have the wood against the teeth and not just the body of the blade). Slide the miter gauge up until it's resting against the apron. At the other end of the apron,

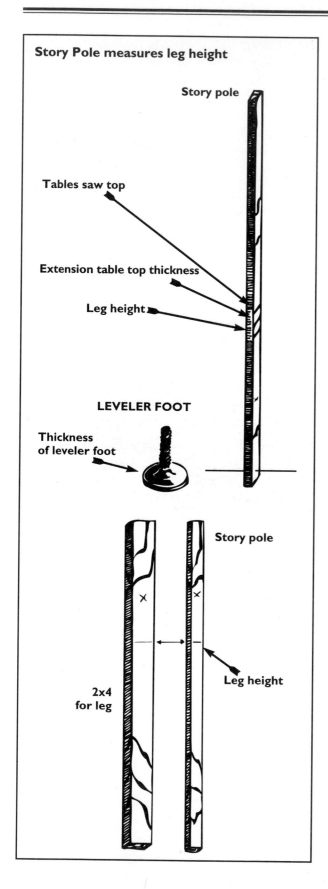

Story Pole measures leg height

Story pole

Tables saw top

Extension table top thickness

Leg height

LEVELER FOOT

Thickness of leveler foot

Story pole

2x4 for leg

Leg height

clamp a small block of wood against the apron and miter-gauge extension. Remove the apron end. You now have an accurate measurement for milling the remaining apron end. This type of transfer of measurement can be used for any board that doesn't go beyond the miter-gauge extension.

10. Place the remaining apron end against the stop block and cut it to length.

11. Dry-clamp the apron ends in place. If you are using a door, treat the apron ends as you did the sides; place 1x2s underneath the table for the clamps to rest on. With particleboard this isn't necessary.

12. Leave one apron side clamped in place and remove the rest. If you leave one apron side in place, then you won't have to go to the trouble of re-positioning the entire apron. Also, the apron side you have left in place will be the first to be glued into place.

Constructing the legs

PAM: Transfer the leg-height measurement with a 1x2 story pole. I find that using a story pole is more accurate and easier than using a tape measure. The tape always seems to flop around, and all those little lines can really get confusing. And, if you're anything like me, you immediately forget the measurement you just took. Forget all that nonsense, and transfer measurements whenever you can.

To figure the leg height, use this formula: The table saw/extension table height minus the thickness of the extension table top minus the leg leveler and tee nut equals the leg height. Before you begin, set a piece of wood on top of the table saw to use as a guide—measuring off the rails isn't accurate enough.

1. Set the story pole against the table saw. On the pole, mark the height of the table (this is the bottom edge of the board lying

across the table saw). Don't forget to mark the story pole for direction—draw an arrow underneath the line pointing up. On more than one occasion I've marked a pole correctly, but forgot the arrow and cut a board to the wrong end of the pole.

2. Run over to your extension table top. Align the table saw height line with the extension table top and mark the thickness of the extension table onto the pole (you should be heading toward the floor at this point). Cross out the table saw height line, and label the new height mark.

3. Place a leg leveler on the line, mark its length, and add no more than $1/4$ in. for the tee nut. Mark the story pole for the new leg height, crossing out all the old lines, so you don't get confused. And there you have it, the leg height.

4. Transfer the leg height mark on the story pole to a piece of 2x4 leg stock; put an X (for reference) on the side that is considered waste. This is a good habit to get into. If you mark everything, you will always have a reference as to which side of the line to cut on.

5. Crosscut the legs. Working with a 2x4x10 or even a 2x4x8 is cumbersome, if not dangerous. I rough out long lumber to a more manageable length first on either the table saw or with the jig saw.

6. Set the blade height for 2x4 lumber.

7. Align the pencil mark with the kerf cut on the miter extension. Be careful what side of the line you are cutting on; you want the full leg length, not the leg minus the kerf. At this point it's not that critical—the levelers will compensate for mistakes (to a certain degree). However, in the future, on more precise projects, kerf cuts become crucial.

Align the leg height mark with the kerf cut on the miter-gauge extension.

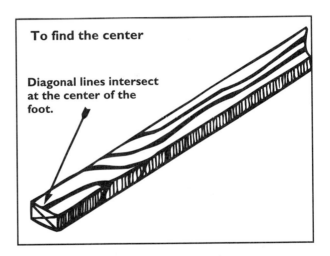

To find the center

Diagonal lines intersect at the center of the foot.

Leg levelers and tee nuts level a table or bench on an uneven floor.

8. Crosscut the leg. Double-check the leg with the story pole to make sure you have milled it to the correct measurement.

9. Using the leg you have just cut as a reference, set up a stop block to mill the remaining three legs. If you have forgotten how to set a stop block on the miter extension, refer to Step 9 in "Constructing the Apron."

10. Crosscut the remaining legs to length.

Leg levelers

PAM: You set the levelers into the bottom of each leg by drilling a hole in the bottom of the leg, tapping a tee-nut over the hole, and screwing in the leveler.

1. Find the center of the bottom of a leg. You can eyeball this, as it doesn't matter if it's off a bit, or you can draw two lines from opposite corners—where they cross is the center.

2. Clamp down the leg for drilling. To figure out which drill bit to use for the tee-nut, place a bit through the threaded tee-nut hole; when you've found a bit that fits snugly, use the next size larger. You don't want the hole too tight, otherwise adjusting the leveler will be difficult, but don't make it too loose either. Drill the hole deep enough so the entire leveler bolt can screw down tightly on the tee-nut if necessary.

3. Tap the leg on the floor to remove any sawdust from the hole. Tap in the tee-nut with a hammer, so that the hole in the tee-nut and the hole in the leg align. Screw in the leveler.

4. Repeat these steps for each leg.

Woodworking Adhesives

PAUL: Before you start assembling the pieces of this project, let me tell you some things about glue, so that you'll have a fighting chance at success. There are many adhesives on the market today, but only a few can be used for woodworking.

Woodworking glues are formulated to bond wood cells to each other. Bonding occurs when two boards are brought together under pressure (as with clamps); the adhesive is forced into the open cells, and the moisture in the glue is absorbed by the surrounding cells, which cures the glue and mechanically bonds the boards together.

Yellow glue and white glue are not the same. White glue, or craft glue as most people know it, will bond wood together, but it is too flexible for good adhesion. Plus, it doesn't sand well since it heats up and clogs the abrasive.

Yellow glue is similar to white glue, except it contains aliphatic resins, which increase strength and moisture resistance; yellow glue also sands better than white glue. Always choose yellow over white glue for woodworking. Yellow glue has a shelf life of about one year, after which it becomes thick and stringy and should be discarded. Neither yellow or white glue can stand freezing; if frozen, the glue will become chalky and usually will not set up. If it does set up, it will dry opaque white; the squeeze-out will stay in the wood pores like paint, and can be removed only by sanding down to the next layer of cells.

Yellow glue has about a five-minute open-coat time—this is how much time you have to get the boards clamped together before the glue starts to set up. Its clamping time is about 20 to 30 minutes, and then the clamps can be removed. The glue is dry in about an hour, but should be allowed to cure for at least 24 hours before sanding or planing the joints.

Polyurethane wood glue—Pam and I came across a glue at a woodworking show that has solved a lot of problems Pam had when gluing a number of boards together all at once. By the time she had spread yellow glue on all the edges and got the boards aligned and clamped, the glue was setting up and the bonds were weak, or not holding at all. The glue that we recommend for beginners, or for any woodworker who has numerous pieces to bond all at once, is polyurethane wood glue. It has an open-coat time of about 20 minutes, which is adequate to position the pieces before the glue starts to set. The drawback here is that the clamp time is 1 to 4 hours—at least—but the glue is totally cured in 24 hours.

Polyurethane glue will not freeze, and it has limited shelf life (about 6 months,) so don't buy a huge bottle unless you are planning to build numerous projects—quickly. Also, once the glue dries on your hands, you won't get it off. Before it dries, remove it with denatured alcohol.

Gluing technique—Using glue properly takes time and experience. Pam can attest to this. When she first started gluing boards together, the woodworking adhesives manufacturers' stock went through the roof. Pam subscribed to the widely held theory that if a little is good, a lot is better...she's still scraping glue off the floor.

Glue should be applied to the board so the edge is completely covered and wet when the boards are clamped together. You can apply it with a brush, rubber roller, or finger—I have been spreading yellow glue with my fingers for years; this way I can control the thickness of the glue line, I can tell when the glue is starting to tack (dry out), and I can control any overflow. Although many glue labels tell you to cover both surfaces before mating, I don't find this necessary. And if the label tells you that the glue will hold end-grain pieces together, don't believe it. The glue will be sucked into the

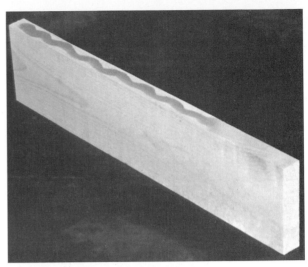

Squiggle a bead of glue down the middle of the board's edge, then spread it out evenly from side to side.

An even bead of glue squeezeout indicates the proper amount of glue.

open end-grain pores, resulting in a weak joint that will eventually fail.

When spreading glue, make sure the mating surfaces are clean. Apply a thin bead of glue down the center of the edge of the board; then, working quickly, spread the glue evenly over the surface, using a side-to-side swiping motion, starting at the center and working toward the edges.

For even pressure on the glue line, alternate clamps so one is above the work, the next is below the work, the next is above, and so on. If the joints fit tightly, apply enough pressure to create an even glue bead; the excess glue that squeezes out will bead evenly down the joint seam. If the joint has small gaps, you'll need more pressure to draw the boards together; if the gaps are wide, the joint will probably fail over time. Beware applying too much pressure—the glue will mostly squeeze out, resulting in a "starved" joint that will fail when the clamps are removed. I use this rule of thumb: Tighten the clamp until snug, then give the handle an extra tweak, but don't go past a quarter-turn.

What to do with the extra glue—Yellow glue will clean up with water while it's still liquid. But I don't recommend wiping off extra glue, because all this does is to force the glue into the pores of the wood, making it impossible to sand out. Instead, ignore the glue, no matter how much it bothers you. Glue requires pressure to bond, remember? So if it's just sitting there on the board, it's not bonding. After the glue has dried, remove it with a paint scraper. Scrape in the direction of the grain. If you go across the grain, the scraper can tear out the wood. Naturally, you don't want a lot of glue leaking down the boards, but it can't be helped until you get the feel of how much glue to use.

Glue holding power—Glue is strong stuff; aliphatic glue is about seven times stronger than the wood on an edge or face joint. Once the glue sets, you aren't going to be able to break a joint apart, at least not at the glue line.

Gluing the apron

PAUL: The apron is glued up one piece at a time. Before you start gluing, make sure you have everything at hand. Set out the clamps—you need one per foot. If you don't have that many, the maximum you can go is a clamp per 1-$^1/_2$ ft., but this will result in a weaker joint. Place the clamps right next to where you will be working and unplug the phone. Check the label on the glue bottle for the set-up time, to see how long you should leave the clamps in place. Read through all instructions before you begin—once you start gluing, you don't have time to stop. Clamp pressure is important: Don't overtighten. On the other hand, you don't want the clamp just barely holding the pieces together. Tighten until you feel resistance, then go about a quarter- turn more.

The apron will be glued in this order: Side, end, end, final side. Glue is slippery, and boards will slide out of position when you clamp them. Use an indexing stick to block the board so it stays in place.

1. With the apron side still dry-clamped in place, set the 1x2 (now referred to as the indexing stick) right behind the apron and clamp the indexing stick to the ends of the table. Mark the ends of the apron on the

Align the apron with the pencil marks.

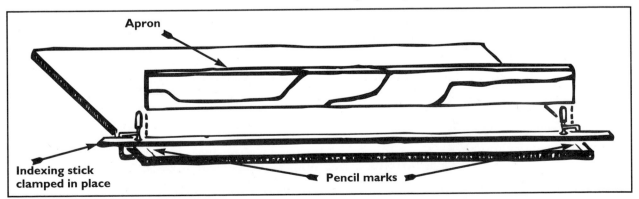

Once the apron is clamped in place, remove the indexing stick so it doesn't get glued to the table.

Glue the apron ends in place with pipe clamps.

table; when you remove the apron, you need a reference where to reposition the ends.

2. Remove the apron, run a bead of glue down the edge, and spread it around.

3. Set the apron side in place against the indexing stick and align it with the pencil marks.

4. Start clamping in the middle and work your way down the apron to one end. Then go back to the middle and clamp to the other end. Place every other clamp in the opposite direction, that is, one going up, then one going down.

5. Once the last clamp is set, remove the indexing stick to keep it from gluing to the table.

6. Wait for the glue to dry before removing the clamps from the apron.

7. Dry-clamp the remaining apron pieces in position. Use the second apron side as an indexing stick to align the apron ends.

8. If the top of your table is a hollow-core door, position an indexing stick underneath the table for the clamps to rest on. If the top is particleboard, you can clamp directly to it.

9. Remove the apron ends, then glue on one end at a time. Besides running a bead of glue down the edge, also apply a bead of glue on the surface that will mate with the apron side that is already glued into place.

Use the last apron side to align the apron ends.

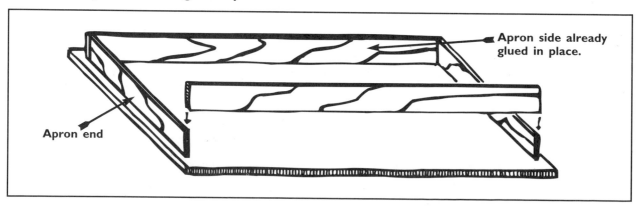

Apron side already glued in place.

Apron end

10. Clamp the end into place.

11. Glue and clamp the remaining end.

12. Remove the apron side that is acting as the indexing stick. Place a pipe clamp across the length of the apron end and clamp to the glued side; this draws the two boards tightly together.

13. Run a bead of glue down the edge of the final apron side; also put a glue bead on the apron ends (where the apron ends meet the apron side). Clamp the apron side to the table, and set a pipe clamp across the ends.

Installing the legs

1. Set a leg into place against the corner of the apron. Mark a line on the leg where it meets the bottom of the apron; this tells you where to spread the glue.

2. Spread glue between the end of the leg and the pencil line.

3. Clamp the leg in place.

4. Glue and clamp the remaining legs.

Finishing

PAM: When the glue has cured, upright the table and admire it! You're not done though—you still have another table to build, and you should finish the surface of the one you just completed. I'm not talking about a major finishing job here, but it's a good place to experiment if you are so inclined. You want a slick, smooth surface for boards to slide across, as well as one that will keep glue drips from subsequent projects from being absorbed by the table top. At least give the top a couple of coats of a good wax, the stuff you buy at the woodworking store (with a high carnauba wax content), not the stuff you buy in the supermarket. Rewax the top every six or seven months. You

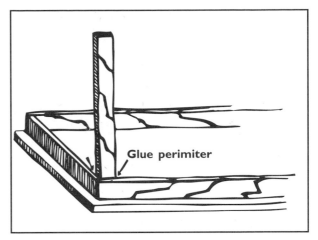

Draw the glue perimeter on the leg.

Set the leg in place against the apron. Use two clamps—one clamp draws the leg to the apron side, the other draws the leg to the apron end.

don't have to worry about the rest of the table. If you used a door for the top, sand it before waxing. Particleboard doesn't need sanding, but do wax it. I had polyurethane left over from another project and used that on my table tops, followed by a coat of wax.

Pushsticks

PAUL: You can make 'em, you can buy 'em, but whatever you do, use 'em. Are you in a quandary as to how to get that board past the saw guard or hold-down wheels without getting your fingers near the blade? Pushsticks! Pushsticks! Pushsticks!

Pushsticks are mainly used in ripping to finish the cut, but they are also used with a router table to push thin boards past the bit. Yes, you can go out and purchase them, but it's more convenient to make your own. Tailor the pushstick to meet your needs; big, thick pushblocks for larger stock, tall, thin sticks for narrow stock.

Baltic birch plywood is the best material, but solid scrap lumber works, too—don't choose any having spits, checks, or knots. Don't use fiberboard or particleboard, not even for a quick fix; neither of these materials will hold up to the stress and will break in your hand during use—a nasty experience.

The key to a good pushstick is the hook on the bottom that fits over the board. I have used pushblocks with foam-rubber pads on the bottom instead of a hook—the pad is supposed to grip the board, but it doesn't. Another critical feature is the handle, which should have a slight forward angle. The angle is not just for comfort; an angled handle will keep the momentum forward and reduce the tendency to tilt the pushstick back off the board.

If your saw is equipped with a table-saw guard, you can use any type of pushstick. Hold-down wheels, however, require the use of rather long, thin pushsticks, since you have to be able to get the foot underneath the wheels. The front hold-down wheel should be set as close to the blade as possible, but not overlapping it, which will cause kickback. Make sure the wheel isn't set too far back—you will have to reach over the wheel with your pushstick to finish the cut, and this isn't safe.

Making a pushstick for use with hold-down wheels

PAUL: Cut the entire pushstick out of one sheet of plywood with a jigsaw. It's much easier than trying to glue and clamp the handle to the foot.

1. Pencil the pushstick outline on the plywood.

Hook fits over board edge.

Pushstick for use with hold-down wheels has angled handle.

Pushblock foot grabs board.

2. Cut out the pushstick with a jigsaw or a coping saw. If you are using the jigsaw, and trying to cut a tight radius, go slow.

3. With sandpaper, round over the handle edges for comfort.

Building a pushblock

PAUL: Always glue the pieces of a pushblock together. Never use screws, because they could damage your sawblade.

1. Make the base (the piece the foot and handle are attached to), from 1x4 scrap lumber. Crosscut the base to about 6 in.

2. Make the foot by crosscutting a $^1/_2$-in. to $^3/_4$-in. strip off a 1x4. The length of the foot should equal the width of the base. Glue and clamp the foot to the base.

3. Cut out the shape of the handle from plywood (baltic birch is nice) with a jigsaw. Sand the edges smooth for a comfortable grip.

4. Glue and clamp the handle to the top of the pushblock.

Jigsaw Safety

PAUL: You should have already read about safety in your owner's manual. Here are a few additional pointers.

In a sense, this is a blind cut, that is, you can't see where the blade is exiting. Therefore, your fingers and hands should not support the work—period. If you're hanging onto a board and cutting it at the same time, you might cut your fingers off. Use extension tables or sawhorses to support the work. Make sure the surfaces supporting the work are out of line with the cut; otherwise you just might trim off the side of your extension table.

Before you turn on the jigsaw, place the base firmly on the work; however, you don't want the blade in contact with the work until after you turn on the jigsaw.

If you're not cutting all the way through (the cut stops before reaching the end of the work), back up the blade a bit so it's not in contact with the work, turn off the saw, and don't lift the machine until the blade has

come to a complete stop. If you try to lift a jigsaw out of the cut while the blade is coming to a halt, you will bend or break the blade, or worse, lose control of the machine.

If you are cutting all the way through, finish the cut, shut off the jigsaw, keep the machine away from your body, and wait for the blade to come to a complete stop before setting it down. Don't just shut it off and toss it aside. You never know what it might come in contact with, and you better hope it's not your person.

Remember always to unplug a machine when you are working on it or changing its blade. Use the proper blade for the intended cut, and make sure the blade is secure in the blade clamp. If you are going to cut tight corners, get a blade that will cut tight curves; these are very thin blades. If you try to cut too short a radius with a regular blade, you stand a chance of binding or bending the blade.

7 THE WORKBENCH

> ## NOT A QUICK PROJECT
> This bench is not a weekend project. It will probably take one or two months to build, depending on your schedule and how many mistakes you make. Don't be fooled (as I initially was) by the craftsmen on television, who give the illusion that it's possible to turn out an entire entertainment center/bedroom set in about half an hour.

PAM: Every woodworker wants to start out making something big and impressive. Forget those measly tie racks and key holders. You didn't purchase a table saw for puny work. What to do about that large-furniture desire? Make a workbench. You need one of these anyway, and the work is fairly easy—if you follow our directions. And so what if you bungle a few things, it's your bench, not something you're going to display in the dining room. When I started woodworking, I didn't have a bench. Instead, I used my antique Brunswick pool table, until I got worried about cracking the slate. Once I had a bench, I wondered how I had lived without it.

Of course, you could always purchase a bench, but then you would be defeating the purpose of this book. Quite frankly, your

This workbench with woodworker's vise features a ledged shelf (to keep things from falling off) and a tool tray to hold small items.

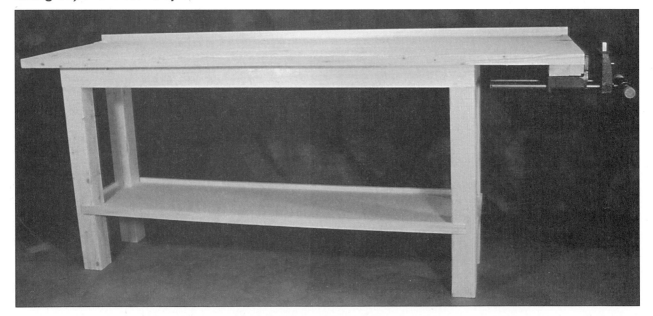

money would be better spent on a planer and drill press than a workbench.

As with the extension tables discussed in the previous chapter, dimensions here are relative. You can make the bench as big or as small as you want. So that you will know how much lumber to buy, we will walk you through each part of the table and show you how to measure it. Your shop might not accommodate the workbench I made. Mine is very tall, because I'm tall, and the table top is 7-1/2 ft. long—I had the room. You might design a bench that's much smaller, or maybe you want a bench that is 3 ft. longer—it's up to you. But whatever you do, make the bench long enough to support whatever type of vise you buy.

The Workbench Design

PAUL: Before finalizing the dimensions of your bench, you have to decide on your vise and the material you'll use for the top. First the vise.

Start with your vise

PAUL: Woodworking vises come in different sizes. Make sure to get a vise made for woodworking; this type of vise has a movable stop that when pushed up is used in conjunction with bench dogs (stops) to brace the wood you are working on. When you don't need to use the vise stop, it's pushed down flush with the top of the jaws. You'll need to check with your local woodworking store or woodworker's catalog to determine which size of vise is best for you. While a small vise will do the same as a large vise when it comes to bracing wood, it won't perform some other tasks. For instance, I clamp my belt sander in my vise and use it as a stationary tool; when you have many small parts to sand, it's easier to clamp the belt sander down than to clamp each piece of wood.

The length of the rails to which the front jaw is attached will determine how deeply the bench apron should be inset from the bench

A woodworker's bench vise has an movable stop at the top of the jaw against which you can brace the wood you're working on.

top. A small vise might take up only 6 in. or so underneath the bench for the rails; a large vise might take 12 to 14 in. for rails and clearance.

I prefer a rapid-action vise; this vise is unscrewed half a turn or so and then pulled out, or pushed back, to the length you need. With a regular vise, the jaws are screwed back and forth to adjust to whatever is being clamped. Pulling the vise jaws back and forth is faster than screwing them back and forth. At this point, that might not sound like a big deal, but if you use your vise a lot, you will appreciate a rapid-action vise.

The workbench top

PAM: The size of the top determines the other dimensions of the bench. Two good choices are a hardwood solid-core door, or pine 2x4s edge-glued together. If you go for the door, try to find a salvaged one—it will be less expensive but plenty durable. Just make sure it has a smooth, unpatterned surface. Remember that you can rip a solid-core door to any size, unlike a hollow-core door.

A top made from edge-glued 2x4s can be a bit cheaper than a solid-core hardwood door, depending on the size of the bench, but it will take longer to build. Since this is a book about learning, the experience you gain from handling, ripping, gluing, and finishing the wood will be invaluable—the more you do something, the more knowledge you acquire. Yet there are some disadvantages with this type of top. First, there is more building involved: 2x4s have eased edges that have to be ripped off, and the boards have to be edge-glued together. Second, there will be a fair amount of sanding required to level the top. And third, pine is soft, and unless you finish the top with something tough, such as spar varnish, you will mar the surface every time you hit it.

If you're using a solid-core hardwood door, just figure out what size you want. If you're making a 2x4 top, remember that a 2x4 actual-

ly measures 3-1/2 in. wide, not a full 4 in. After you rip 1/4 in. off each edge, you'll end up with a finished dimension of 3 in. per piece. Use this information when calculating how many 2x4s it will take to create the desired width, and don't forget to add 20 percent for waste—2x4s have a nasty way of warping as they acclimate to the warmth and dryness of a shop interior. I bought nine 2x4s for my bench top but ended up using only seven, which gave me a total finished width (after the eased edges were ripped off) of 21-1/2 in.

Sizing the rest of the bench

PAM: Legs, apron, cleats, shelf, shelf ledge, and tool tray are all milled from dimensional pine. Take rough, not exact, measurements; when you're a beginner, it's a good idea to give yourself some leeway. Sure, you end up with waste, but save the wood to be used on other projects. As you get more proficient in woodworking, you will start figuring to exact measurements.

The legs—You'll need four of these, made from 4x4 lumber. To determine leg height, measure to your waist and drop down a couple of inches. Is that a comfortable height? If not, adjust accordingly; if you have a table in your house that you work on and like, use that leg height. Another hint: How do you like your extension table height? Use that for a reference if it's working for you.

To calculate the amount of lumber you'll need, take this example: Suppose you wanted the bench legs 35 in. high. Multiply that number by four legs and you get 140 in., or 11.6 ft. Since 12-ft. lumber is a hassle to handle, buy two 4x4x8-ft. boards and have scrap.

The apron—The apron consists of two sides and two ends, made from 1x4 lumber. To make this easy, and also to give you some room for waste, figure the apron measurements to be the same as the finished bench top, minus the

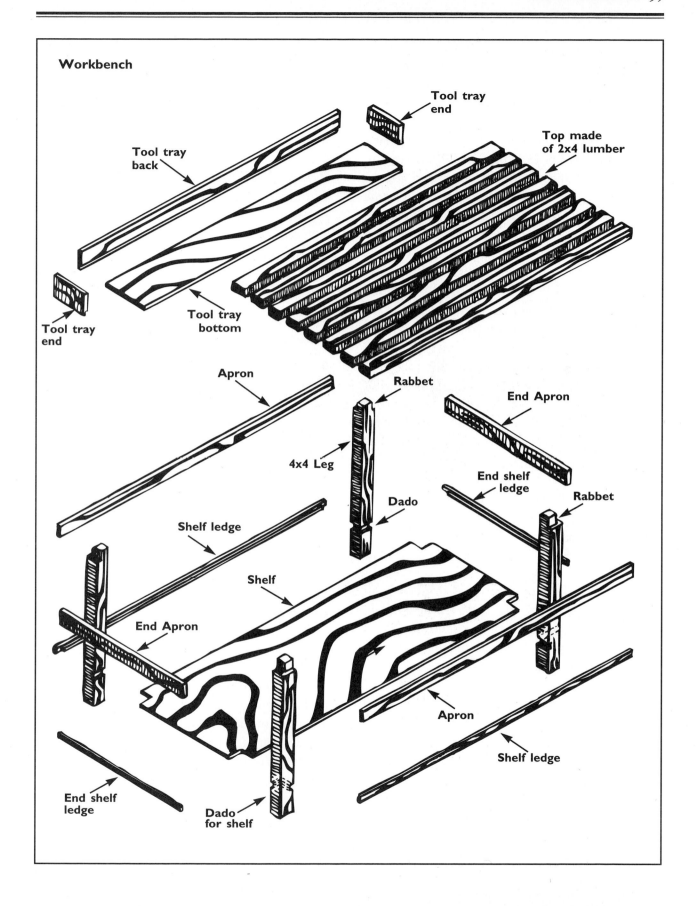

Workbench

Tool tray end

Tool tray back

Top made of 2x4 lumber

Tool tray bottom

Tool tray end

Apron

Rabbet

4x4 Leg

Dado

End Apron

End shelf ledge

Rabbet

Shelf ledge

Shelf

End Apron

Apron

End shelf ledge

Dado for shelf

Shelf ledge

space taken up by the length of the vise rails. Although the apron will not be installed flush with the edges of the bench, right now this is an easy way to get the measurements.

The cleats—You'll need two sides and two ends, made from 1x2 lumber. The cleats are edge-glued to the apron; the bench top attaches to the cleats. Make the cleat ends the same length as the apron ends and the cleat sides the same length as the apron sides.

The shelf—Use ³/₄-in. thick particleboard for the shelf (anything thinner will sag). The shelf acts as a stretcher, which stabilizes the piece and keeps it from wobbling. The shelf dimension is the same as the apron dimension. You will have to buy a 4x8 sheet of particleboard and rip it down—this will leave you with a lot of leftover particleboard, but you can use it up when you make the top for the router table. Particleboard is heavy stuff, and some lumberyards will rip it for you to make it easier to handle. Just make sure there's a piece large enough for the shelf.

The shelf ledge—This is made from 1x2 lumber, and consists of two ends and two sides. Not only does a shelf ledge look nice, it keeps stuff from falling off the shelf, hides rough edges, and prevents the shelf from sagging. Make the end shelf ledges the same length as the apron ends, and the side shelf ledges the same length as the apron sides.

The tool tray—Make the back from 1x4 lumber, the bottom from 1x8 lumber. While you don't absolutely need a tool tray, it's sure nice to have. It keeps chisels from falling on the floor, and holds all your pencils, glue bottles, and various other items you need at hand. Both the back and bottom of the tool tray equal the length of the bench, yet both pieces are not the same width; the bottom piece is

twice as wide so that it can be attached underneath the bench. If both pieces were the same width, by the time you got done attaching the tray bottom to the bench, the area that holds your tools and stuff would only be about an inch wide, which isn't wide enough to hold much.

The Bill of Materials and Hardware/Tool List

PAM: Put together your bill of materials, which will also act as your milling list. It should look like this, but with your lumber lengths lengths filled in for the question marks.

Piece	How many	Lumber size
Bench top or	(1)	2 x 4 x (?)
Solid-core door)	(1)	
Legs	(4)	4 x 4 x (?)
Apron ends	(2)	1 x 4 x (?)
Apron sides	(2)	1 x 4 x (?)
Cleat ends	(2)	1 x 2 x (?)
Cleat sides	(2)	1 x 2 x (?)
Shelf-ledge ends	(2)	1 x 2 x (?)
Shelf-ledge sides	(2)	1 x 2 x (?)
Tool-tray bottom	(1)	1 x 8 x (?)
Tool-tray back	(1)	1 x 4 x (?)
Shelf (particleboard)	(1)	³/₄ in. thick

Add to the bill of material:

Miter extensions	(2)	1 x 4 x 8'

One board would probably do, but there is nothing worse than being in the middle of a job and running out of lumber for something. Beside, you can always use a leftover 1x4 on another project.

Story poles	(2 or 3)	1 x 2 x 8'

Got it? Good! Now before you run off to the lumberyard, make a hardware/tool list. This is a list of stuff you need to complete the project. Some items you might have on hand, others you might need to purchase. No sense in making a million trips before you start, or while you're in the middle of assembling the project.

Hardware / Tool List:

- **Quick-action vise**
- **Dado blades and dado throat plate**
- **Handful of 1-5/8-in. drywall or wood screws**
- **Featherboard**
- **1/2-in. dowel for bench dogs**
- **Power drill and bits, countersink bit**
- **Yellow wood glue, polyurethane glue**
- **Pipe clamps—if you are making the 2x4 bench top, you will need to plan for about one clamp per foot. Therefore, if your bench top is 6 ft. long, you will need six pipe clamps.**
- **Bar clamps (6 to 8)**
- **Combination square**
- **Framing square and/or try square**
- **A lot of pencils**

Building the Bench Top

PAM: If you'll be using a door for your bench top, skip these steps and head right for the legs. If you're building the top from 2x4s, read on.

Two things are involved in building the bench top. You'll have to square up the 2x4s by ripping about 1/4 in. off each edge. Then you'll edge-glue the pieces together. Don't try to crosscut the 2x4s to length before edge-gluing. If you do, when gluing the top together, the boards will probably slip out of position. Cut the ends flush later with a jigsaw.

Ripping the 2x4s

PAM: Begin by sorting through your lumber. Lay the 2x4s next to each other, removing any that are badly warped or twisted (don't throw them away, you can cut them up and use them as short lengths for another project). A tiny bit of warp on a 2x4 is almost unavoidable, but any more than a tiny bit and ripping the wood can

get very dangerous, not to mention how the bench top will look once it's glued up. In some cases you will find that a few of the 2x4s are beyond use, and you'll have to go buy more.

1. Set up your extension tables for infeed and outfeed.

2. Set up your rip or combination blade and adjust the blade height. Check the blade for square.

3. If you are using hold-down wheels, adjust the wheels according to the instructions to make sure they're not too loose or too tight. Too tight, and feeding the wood is almost impossible; too loose, and the wheels won't function properly.

4. Adjust the fence so that you aren't ripping off too much—you just want to take off the rounded edge, about 1/4 in.

5. Rip off one edge of each board. This is a production run, so don't rip one edge of a board, flip it over, readjust the fence and rip the other edge. If you do, you'll be at this forever. Rip one edge off each board until all the boards are done. Then and only then readjust the fence and proceed to rip the other edge off each of the boards.

Gluing and clamping

PAM: For this work, use polyurethane glue. Its long open-coat time (20 minutes) will allow you to spread glue from one end of the edge to the other without having to worry about the glue drying before you get the boards clamped. If you haven't already done so, review the glue information in Chapter 6.

When clamping, shoot for one clamp per foot of wood. You can possibly get by with one clamp per foot-and-a-half if you're short on clamps, but never stretch it to one clamp for every two feet—you'll get an inadequate bond.

Before you glue anything together, look at the annual rings on the ends of your boards.

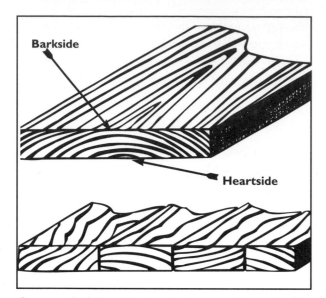

As wood dries, it tends to cup toward the bark side. Alternating the annual rings from board to board will help keep the top flat.

With pine, each ring represents one year of growth. Sometimes boards that are flat-sawn will cup across the grain—the board starts looking like a dish; the wider the board, the more likely it will cup. Therefore, when gluing wide surfaces such as a bench or table top, it's best to use narrow strips to prevent cupping.

Another procedure that helps eliminate cupping is to alternate the annual rings. When you lay out the boards this way, mark the surface of each board as to which way it goes. I put a couple of Xs on the surface that faces the floor.

You'll have more control if you glue the 2x4s in pairs, then glue the pairs together. Use your extension tables to support the boards. If some of your boards are warped—and chances are all your boards aren't perfectly straight—you can attempt to straighten out the warp when you glue the boards together. Start in the middle, and as you clamp the boards together, either pull up on one board, or push the other board down. If the board is severely warped, discard it and mill another board to take its place. Trying to glue a very warped board will create undue stress, a weak joint and a warped top.

Time to get gluing:

1. Select two boards and set out the clamps. Run a bead of glue down the edge of one board and spread it around, covering the entire surface.

2. Slide the mating boards together. Start clamping in the middle and work your way to each end. Be sure to alternate the clamps so one is on top, the next underneath, and so on. If you put all the clamps on top, the boards might cup. Use clamp blocks to keep from denting the milled edges with the clamp jaws.

3. After the glue has set (check the bottle for set-up time) and you have removed the clamps, scrape off the excess glue with a paint scraper being careful not to gouge the soft pine.

4. Repeat these steps until you have glued all the 2x4s into pairs.

5. Glue the pairs together. Use the pipe clamps—they are stronger and give greater stability when spanning distances. Even if your bar clamps will reach across the 2x4s, if the distance is greater than 18 in., when pressure is applied to the clamp the bar will start to bend, which means you are losing pressure, and if the clamp won't apply adequate pressure, you won't get a tight glue joint.

6. When the bench top is complete, figure out which side you want facing up and which side should face the floor. Set the benchtop on two sawhorses, with the good side facing the floor. From here on out, you will be building the bench upside down.

Trimming the top to length

PAM: You need to square the staggered ends, so figure out how much you want to take off. Whatever it is, you also need to compensate for the jigsaw foot; you want the entire foot on the bench. If you only have part of the foot on the bench, and the other part hanging out in the breeze, it will be difficult to brace the jigsaw for a straight cut. And be sure to trim both ends of the bench, not just one.

1. At the edge, pencil a mark at the desired length for the bench top. Use a framing square or a long straight board to extend the mark to the opposite edge.

2. Set the jigsaw blade on the pencil mark. Pencil another mark at the edge of the jigsaw foot. Repeat on the opposite edge.

3. Clamp a fence to the jigsaw foot mark—a straight 1x4 will do.

4. Crosscut the end of the bench top.

5. Repeat these steps on the other end of the bench top.

When trimming the top to length, allow for the foot of the jigsaw when locating the guide fence.

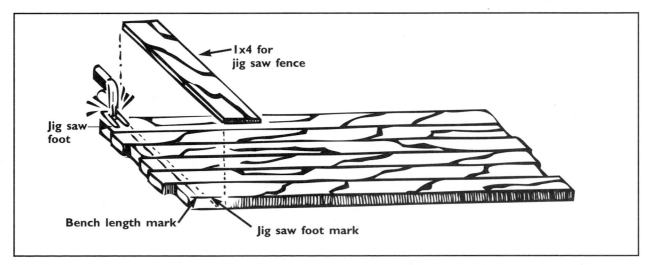

1x4 for jig saw fence

Jig saw foot

Bench length mark

Jig saw foot mark

To square the miter gauge, remove the extension, loosen the miter gauge, turn it over and set the bar in the ways. Push the miter gauge against the table saw. Tighten the miter gauge.

Milling The Legs

PAM: If you are using a door for the bench top, support it on sawhorses with the best side facing the floor.

The dimensions for the rest of the bench are taken from the relationship of the bench top to the legs. This gives you a bit of flexibility. Nothing is set in stone and you can adjust dimensions as you go along.

When using a dado blade, or whenever sawing in a way in which you don't saw all the way through a board, you are making a "blind cut," that is, you can't see where the blade is as it passes through and then exits the wood. This doesn't create problems when you first start the cut. However, when the blade exits the lumber, if you have a finger or thumb in the way, it will get chopped off. Be very careful with blind cuts. Once I have my miter extension in place, but before I set up any wood for milling, I like to run the miter extension through the blade. The kerf created by the blade gives me a reference as to where the blade will exit, and I make sure all appendages are well out of the way. Check the

miter gauge for square before using it, and then periodically throughout the project.

The first thing to do is to cut the 4x4s for the legs to a more manageable length; cut the lumber in half, unless you are milling three legs out of one board, in which case you're stuck with the long length until you get the first leg cut. A 4x4 is cut in two passes, since a table saw blade won't adjust that high.

Suppose you can't get a flat bottom on the leg, and there is a little ledge on the bottom that just won't come off? Unfortunately, if the lumber has a tiny bit of warp in it, and that's all it takes, a tiny bit, that ledge is here to stay. Another problem could be that the miter gauge is out of square—check it against the table saw. Or perhaps the blade isn't square to the table. Check your blade and miter gauge first, and if they are square, you'll just have to live with the slight ledge.

Follow these steps to mill the legs:

1. If you were using a rip blade, replace it with a combination or crosscut blade.

2. Adjust the height of the blade to just a little over half of the thickness of the 4x4.

3. Place the extension tables so they support the 4x4.

4. Use a miter-gauge extension to support the wood through the cut. The extension should span the distance of the table—on both sides of the blade. Use a 6- or 8-ft. long 1x4. Don't place it directly in the center of the table, instead, give yourself 1 ft. to 2 ft. more on the miter-gauge side for balance and support.

5. Mark the leg for height. The first leg is the hardest because you have to realign it with the kerf to make the second cut.

6. Make the first crosscut to the leg.

7. With your try-square, extend down the kerf lines so that you have a reference.

8. Make the second crosscut.

9. Check to see if you have milled the correct height.

10. Set a stop block. If you have forgotten how to do this, refer to Chapter 6.

11. Crosscut the remaining legs to height.

Cutting rabbets and dadoes

PAUL: The legs are rabbeted to accept the apron. The shelf rests in a dado milled in the legs. A rabbet is a recess milled on the edge of a board, and it only has one shoulder. A dado is a recess with two shoulders. In this case, we are going to create these joints using dado blades.

Setting up the dado blades—If you measure the thickness of the 1x4 apron lumber, you will see that it is $\frac{3}{4}$ in. thick. The thickness for the particleboard shelf should be the same. Stack the dado set to this dimension. You should have two outside blades plus chippers for the inside. On the outside blades, you might have gaps for the chippers or you might not. If you don't, then set the chippers in a gullet. Set the first two chippers at 90 degrees to each other, then fill in the gaps with the rest of the chippers. Stacking the set this way balances the blades and makes for a smoother cut; it's easier on the wood, and it's easier on the saw. For a $\frac{3}{4}$-in. dado, I use four of my chippers (each $\frac{1}{8}$ in. wide) between my two outside blades. If you are unsure of the dimensions of your blades and are using a stacked set, then measure the width of the chipper blank (body of the chipper) and a tooth on each outside blade; add up the measurements and stack accordingly. If you are using a wobble dado blade, follow the instructions that came with the blade.

It is impossible to stack a set of dado blades and then slide them on the arbor with-

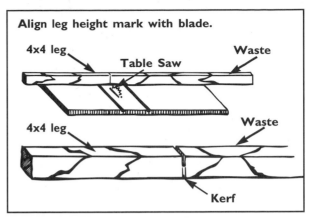

Align leg height mark with blade.

Cut the 4x4 leg to length on the table saw. You'll probably have to turn the wood over and make a second pass. Use your try square to extend the saw kerf and align the cuts.

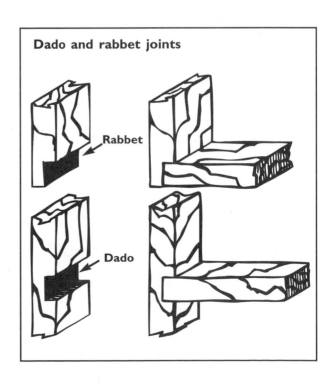

Dado and rabbet joints

out everything slipping apart. Instead, raise the arbor all the way up and stack the set on the arbor. Then tighten the arbor nut. Make sure the chippers haven't shifted, lower the blade, and set the dado throat plate into place. To check the width, adjust the blade height to about ¼ in. and run a scrap piece of lumber through the blades. Adjust accordingly if you don't get a ¾-in. dado.

Go slow when using dado blades. The blades remove a lot of wood at once, and the chippers have only two teeth, each cleaning out the center. If you hear a lot of noise coming from the throat plate area, you are feeding the wood too quickly.

Rabbeting the legs for the apron

PAUL: Each leg is rabbeted on two sides to accept the apron.

1. To transfer the width of the apron to the leg, place the apron lumber across the leg, making sure that the leg and apron lumber are flush at the top, and mark the width on the leg. Put a big X in the area that is to be rabbeted.

2. Set the dado blade height. Since you are recessing the apron flush into the leg, you want the rabbet the same depth as the apron lumber thickness. Set the edge of the apron against the dado blade and adjust the blade height flush with the top of the board.

3. Take a piece of wood and set it against the edge of the dado blade. Align the pencil mark for the rabbet with the edge of the board that is resting against the blade. Make sure the blades are heading into the rabbet, not down the leg.

4. Rig the fence as a stop block for the rabbets. This is a bit different from other stop block procedures. When I first showed Pam this technique, it made the hair on the back of

Layout the rabbet by transferring the width of the apron to the leg.

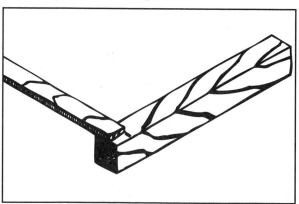

her neck stand on end. You can't use the miter gauge and fence together, not at the same time, she said. Correct, I replied, if you are cutting all the way though the wood. But a dado doesn't cut all the way through the wood. The problem with using a fence that has a stop block attached to it is that as soon as the wood leaves the stop block and heads toward the blade, the wood can slip back in the direction of the stop block, creating an uneven dado shelf. However, with my technique, you get accurate rabbet and dado widths.

So here's how you do it: Move the fence over so that it rests against the top of the leg; lock down the fence. If you have to, reposition your miter-gauge extension; you don't want it touching the fence. Instead, position the extension so that it reaches about half the length of the rabbet. Don't put a stop block on the miter extension to lock the leg in place. This will cause binding, and you will get hurt.

5. Make the first cut for the rabbet.

6. Pull the miter extension back toward you and reposition the rabbet. In this case, you will slide the rabbet away from the fence. To remove more wood from the rabbet, realign the board with the dado blades, and make another pass.

7. Make repeated passes until all of the wood has been removed from the rabbet.

8. When you are done with the first rabbet, check the apron to see how it fits. Set the leg into the rabbet; and adjust your fence setting if needed. Better to have one rabbet off than all four legs rabbeted incorrectly.

9. Repeat the previous steps until all the rabbets have been milled.

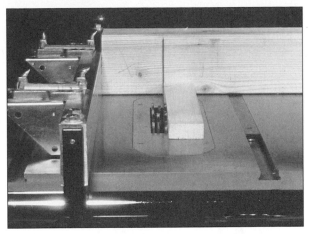

A block of wood aligns the rabbet mark with the outside of the dado blades. When it's right, lock the rip fence against the top of the leg.

Use the miter gauge to make successive cuts with the dado blades until all the wood has been removed from the rabbet.

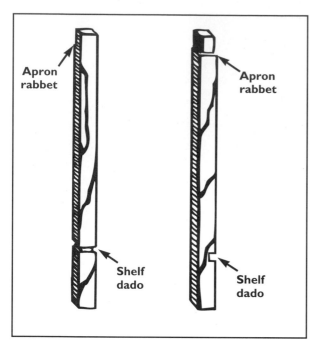

Make the apron rabbets on the two outside faces of the leg. The shelf dadoes are on the two inside faces.

Mill the shelf dados with the bottom of the leg against the fence.

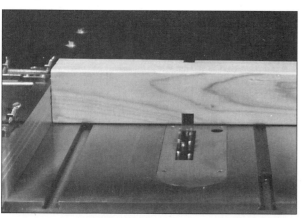

Cutting the shelf dadoes

PAM: Don't touch the blade height; if you are using ³/₄-in. particleboard, it remains the same for the shelf dadoes as for the apron rabbets. (If you are using something else, then you will have to adjust the dado blade width to match the thickness of what you've got. However, the blade height still remains the same.)

1. Figure out how high off the ground you want the shelf. Too high, and you can't stack stuff on it; too low, and you can't stack stuff underneath it. My shelf sits a little over a foot off the ground.

    Note that the dadoes are milled on the opposite side of the rabbets. Place the legs on the bench top with the apron rabbets facing out. The shelf dadoes are milled on the inside of the legs. Mark a line on the leg where you want to position the bottom of the shelf. That mark should not be on a side where there is a rabbet. Put a big X over the area where you are going to make a shelf dado.

2. Line up the pencil mark, dado blades, and fence as discussed previously. It's a good idea to always have the longer part of the stock at the end where you are standing.

3. Before you start milling, look at the leg. Find that X. Make sure the sides with the Xs don't have rabbets. When you set your leg down, the X faces the table. Look at the end of your leg, you should see a rabbet facing up; if you don't, you are milling the wrong side.

4. Mill the dado.

5. Turn the leg to find the remaining X, and place it face down on the table. Again, if you look down the leg, you should see a rabbet. Mill the dado.

6. Dado the remaining legs.

Measuring and Milling the Shelf

PAM: Mill the shelf before the apron pieces. If you mill the apron first, you'll have to cut the shelf to exact dimensions to get it to fit.

1. Set the vise on the bench top—you need to know where the rails end.

2. Set the legs (solid ends, not rabbeted ends, down) on the bench. Position them as shown.

3. Transfer the shelf dimensions with a 1x2 story pole. Lay it on the bench top, one end flush with the outside edge of a leg. At the other end, transfer the outside leg edge to the pole. Label the pole. Repeat with a shorter story pole (it's easier to handle) to transfer the shelf width. Make sure you are transferring the outside edge of the leg to the story pole.

4. Mark the dimensions on the shelf. Unless you had it ripped at the lumberyard, you'll need to rough out the particleboard to manageable size with a jigsaw, before rip-

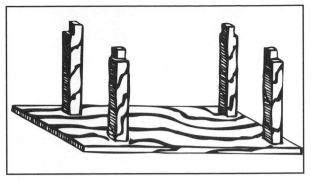

Locate the legs 3 in. to 4 in. away from the edges of the bench top. The extra overhang at the left allows for the vise rails.

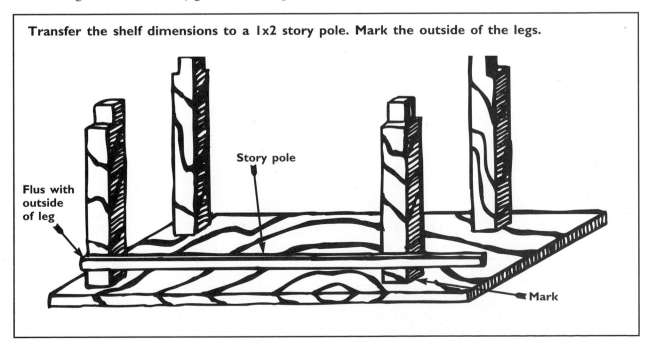

Transfer the shelf dimensions to a 1x2 story pole. Mark the outside of the legs.

Story pole

Flus with outside of leg

Mark

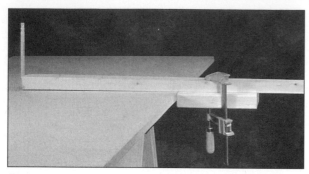

Transfer tool, made from a 1x2, allows you to draw a line far inside a 4x8 sheet of plywood.

ping it on your table saw. Mark the shelf for width first, adding a couple of extra inches. Chances are your combination square won't reach into the sheet that far, so make your own transfer tool, as described in the next step.

5. Place the end of a 1x2 on the width mark for the shelf. The other end of the stick should hang out over the edge. Clamp a block onto the stick, flush against the edge of the particleboard. Use this transfer tool as you would a combination square. Place a pencil at the end, in contact with the particleboard, and run the tool down the sheet.

6. Before cutting the particleboard, position an extension table on either side of the pencil mark. Don't hang the edge of the particleboard over the edge of the extension table. The weight of the particleboard will cause numerous problems once it's partially cut. You want support on both sides of the cut.

7. Cut slowly and carefully down the pencil line with the jigsaw. You don't need to race through this.

8. Position the extension tables for infeed and outfeed with the table saw.

To rip the shelf to its final width, use the shelf width mark on the story pole to set the correct distance between fence and blade.

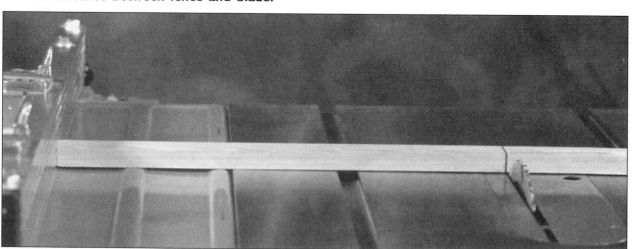

9. Set the table-saw blade height to ¼ in. above the particleboard.

10. Using the story pole shelf-width mark, set the fence into place.

11. Set the straight edge of the particleboard against the fence, not the edge you ripped with the jigsaw. Rip the shelf to width.

12. Don't try and crosscut the shelf to length with the table saw—it's easier and safer with the jigsaw. With the shelf still on the outfeed table, mark it for length with the story pole. Set up a fence as described in steps 2 and 3 of "Trimming the top to length" (p.100).

13. Crosscut the shelf to length. Go slow, and you'll be able to get a fairly accurate, straight cut.

14. To get the shelf to fit flush with the outside of the legs, you have to cut out each corner of the shelf. To determine this measurement, place a rabbeted end of the leg on the corner of the shelf. Mark around the rabbet.

15. Cut out the shelf recess with the jigsaw. Cut away everything but the pencil line.

16. Dry-fit the leg dado into the recess. The shelf should be flush with the outside of the leg.

17. What if the shelf doesn't come all the way out to the edge of the leg? The shelf recess isn't cut deep enough, and that's okay, up to ⅛ in. can be tolerated here since you are going to cover the shelf edge with a ledge.

    What if the shelf goes beyond the leg? The shelf recess was cut too deep. To correct this problem, shim the offending dado, that is, glue thin pieces of wood on the inside of the dado to flush the shelf.

18. Repeat the previous steps for the remaining shelf recesses.

To lay out the shelf recesses, set the leg rabbets flush with each corner of the shelf and draw around them.

Fit the shelf into place and clamp. Measure and crosscut the apron sides; dry-clamp the apron sides in place.

Milling the Apron

PAM: Yes, the apron is much easier and quicker to construct than the shelf. The bench is starting to look like something now, isn't it?

1. Dry-fit the shelf in place. Check for square with your framing square—you don't want the legs flaring out. Clamp into place with a bar clamp across the width.

2. The apron sides are the same length as the shelf. Set your story pole with the shelf-length measurement into place on the rabbets. The mark should line up with the edge of the leg. If it doesn't, check the legs for square and adjust them.

3. Transfer the shelf length mark from the story pole to the apron lumber.

4. Crosscut the apron side to length.

5. Make sure the first apron side fits.

6. If you have a miter extension longer than the apron, set up a stop block. Otherwise, repeat step 3 and crosscut the second apron side to length.

7. Dry-clamp the apron sides in place. The apron ends fit inside the apron sides. Set the end of the story pole against the inside of the apron. Mark the other end to the inside of the apron.

9. Set up a stop block using the story pole-measurement.

10. Crosscut an apron end.

11. Check to see that the apron end fits.

12. Adjust the stop block if necessary, and crosscut the final apron end.

13. Slip both ends into place and dry-clamp.

Gluing Up

PAM: The shelf is glued into the dadoes and then the apron is glued on immediately after. Use polyurethane glue, because it allows plenty of time to shift boards into place before the glue starts drying.

Assembly will be easiest if you work on the floor. Dry- fit all the legs, then take one leg off at a time to spread glue into the shelf dado. Unless you have unions (threaded couplings that connect two pipes of the same dimension together, available in the plumbing section of your home center), for your pipe clamps, you won't be able to clamp the length, so pull and push it together the best you can and then clamp the width.

Clamping the shelf and legs

1. Remove a leg and spread glue in the shelf dado, making sure all surfaces are covered. Slide the leg back into the shelf recess.

2. Do the same to the next leg.

3. When both legs at one end of the bench are glued in place, clamp across the width of the shelf.

4. Repeat the procedure with last two legs.

Assembling the apron

1. Glue one apron piece at a time, starting with the apron side. Spread the glue on the rabbet, not the apron. As you are working along, you might find that the apron doesn't fit. Don't panic, the legs are probably out of square. Clamp one apron end square; go to the other end, and either pull or push the leg to line up with the apron. Clamp the apron to the leg rabbet.

2. Glue the next apron side.

3. Glue the apron ends. Spread the glue over

Glue and clamp the shelf in place, then glue and clamp the apron one piece at a time.

the rabbet, rabbet shoulder, and apron ends. Again, if they don't fit, push the legs apart or pull them together, check for square, and snug the clamp.

4. When the aprons are clamped up, clamp across the width to pull the apron end in tight.

5. After the glue has set up, remove the clamps and clean off excess glue with a paint scraper or sandpaper.

6. Sand the frame if you're so inclined. I prefer to sand as I build, because it saves time later in the project. Paul, on the other hand, sands everything after it is assembled. If you plan to sand now, review the material on abrasives in Chapter 3. Dimensional pine has a fairly smooth surface that doesn't need much work, so don't use anything under 120 grit; if you do, you can end up sanding the wood down to nothing while trying to get rid of the scratch marks left by previous coarser grits. By the same token, don't use anything beyond 150 grit. I wouldn't use a belt sander on pine—no matter what grit you're using. It can really gouge the wood; I know, I've done it plenty of times. Vacuum or dust the wood whenever you change sanding grits.

Cut and attach the cleats

PAM: The cleats are edge-glued to the inside of the apron so the frame can be attached to the top.

1. Place the cleat lumber at the top edge of the apron and inside the leg. Mark the length where the cleat meets the opposite leg. The cleats don't have to fit perfectly flush against the legs. Close is good enough.

Glue and clamp each cleat into place.

2. Crosscut the first cleat.

3. Work around the bench, repeating the previous steps, until all the cleats are cut.

4. Spread yellow glue on the edge of one cleat; you are not face-gluing here. Clamp it against the top inside of the apron. You want it flush with the top edge of the apron.

5. Work your way around the frame until all the cleats are glued into place.

Constructing the shelf ledge and tool tray

PAUL: The shelf ledge and tool tray have rabbets; crosscut both pieces to size first, before putting the dado blades on the saw.

Making the shelf-ledge sides and ends

1. On the leg, mark how far you want the shelf ledge to overlap. Set the combination square to that depth.

2. Mark each side of the leg for a reference position to the shelf ledge.

Use the combination square to locate the ends of the shelf ledges on all four legs.

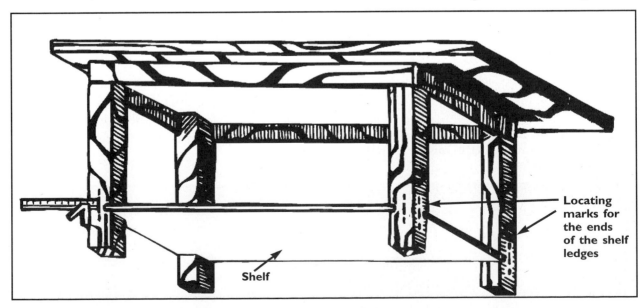

Locating marks for the ends of the shelf ledges

Shelf

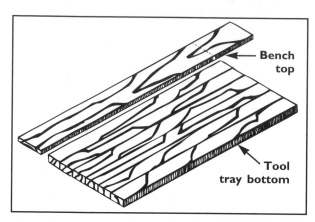

Transfer the length of the bench top to the tool tray bottom.

3. Clamp a ledge across the edge of the shelf, almost to the end of each leg.

4. Place the combination square on the leg and mark the end of the shelf ledge. Do the same to the other end of the shelf ledge.

5. Crosscut the shelf ledge to length.

6. Use the crosscut shelf ledge as a story pole and transfer the length for the next shelf ledge.

7. To make the shelf-ledge ends, repeat steps 3 through 6.

8. Set the shelf ledges aside until later.

Making the tool tray

PAUL: The bottom and the back of the tool tray are the same length as the bench top.

1. Lay the bottom piece for the tool tray next to the bench top; mark the pieces for length.

2. Crosscut the board to length.

3. For the back of the tool tray, repeat steps 1 and 2.

Rabbet for the shelf ledge and tool tray

PAUL: At this juncture, you need a dado-blade auxiliary fence. The rabbets you are going to mill run the length of the board, and in this case, the fence is flush with the outside edge of the dado blade. If you were to do this work without a wood fence, you would chew the heck out of your metal fence. Use a straight 1x4 a little over the length of the metal fence. You can cut down a miter-gauge extension if

The dado blade auxiliary fence, made from a straight 1x4, runs a little longer than the saw's metal rip fence.

you want. However, a 1x4 won't fit underneath Pam's hold-down wheels, so I have to rip the wood to the height of her fence. If you aren't using hold-down wheels, it's okay for the wood to be taller than the metal fence. Here's how to make a dado blade auxiliary fence:

1. Crosscut the 1x4 board a little longer than the length of the metal table-saw fence.

2. If you need to, rip the fence to the height of your metal fence.

3. Screw the wood fence to the tablesaw fence through the screw holes in the back of the metal fence. I use drywall screws, but any wood screw will do. If you don't have screw holes, then clamp the wood fence to the metal fence.

When rabbets run the length of a board...

PAUL: When you use hold-down wheels, there aren't many problems dadoing rabbets until you start working with thin lumber, and then maneuvering a pushstick underneath the wheels can get exciting if it hits the running blades. Hold-downs are great for this type of work, but that doesn't solve the problem of getting the wood past the blades. There are two ways to approach this. The first is, when you get close to the end of the cut, walk around to the back of the saw and pull the wood through. If your hold-downs are properly adjusted, the wood isn't going to go anywhere while you're walking around. The second method is to push the 1x2 past the blades with scrap wood; the scrap should be the same width as the lumber you are rabbeting. I say scrap, because it's going to run through the blades as you push the other piece clear. Once the scrap is under the rear hold-down wheel, you can shut off the saw.

If you aren't using hold-down wheels, you have to use a featherboard. Two are preferable, an infeed and outfeed, with both set close together, the fingers at 45 degrees to the blade. You want to keep the wood snug against the fence going into and leaving the blade.

When rabbeting a thin board with a featherboard setup, use a thin pushstick with a handle (you need the handle for stability). Keep the pushstick on the wood and to the side of where the blades are cutting. If the pushstick is positioned over the rabbet, there is a tendency to push down at the end of the cut, creating a deeper rabbet than you want, and causing possible injury to yourself.

Position the featherboard before the blade height is set. Drop the blades into the table so you have a flush surface. Push the wood against the fence and position the featherboard, pushing the fingers into the board and tightening the featherboard down. You want fairly even pressure on the front and back of the board.

Place the featherboard so that its fingers are parallel to the blade but in advance of it, to help feed the wood.

When rabbeting with a dado blade auxiliary fence, the fence should be right next to, but not touching, the outside dado blade.

The shelf ledge has a rabbet to fit the edge of the shelf, and an end rabbet to fit over the bench leg.

Mark the inside of the shelf ledge against the inside of the leg to show he width of the shelf and create rabbet.

Setting up the dado blades

PAUL: To simplify life, mill all the rabbets ³/₄ in. wide.

1. Mount the dado blades on the arbor and stack to ³/₄-in. wide.

2. Slide the fence over until it touches the outside edge of the dado blade. Then back it off a fraction.

Milling the rabbets

PAUL: All the rabbets are milled at the same height: ³/₈ in. (one-half the thickness of the lumber).

1. Mark the edge of one of the boards for half its thickness. It doesn't have to be exact. If you're off ¹/₁₆ to ¹/₈ in., nobody will notice.

2. Place the board next to the blade and set the blade to the height mark.

3. Adjust the dado-blade height and the featherboard. If you are using featherboards, you have to move the fence to set the height, after the featherboard is in position. Move the fence away from the blade. Follow steps 1 and 2 described previously. Reposition the fence right next to the blade.

4. Mill a rabbet on each shelf ledge piece.

Measuring and cutting the overlap recess

PAUL: The shelf ledge overlaps the legs, for a nice, finished look.

1. Clamp a rabbeted length of shelf ledge in position on the leg marks.

2. Mark the inside of the ledge next to the inside of the leg. You are going to make this recess using the miter gauge and fence, which acts as a stop block. You can use this configuration because you aren't milling all the way through the wood. However, take care how you hold the shelf ledge. You want

it flush on the table surface; since the ledge has been rabbeted, if you push down on the rabbet side, it will tilt and make a real mess of the ledge, not to mention scaring you to death.

3. Align the ledge overlap mark with the outside of the dado blade. Move the fence over to create a stop. Make sure the blades are on the inside of the rabbet, not the outside.

4. Make the first cut.

5. Continue rabbeting the recess. The ledge should be moving away from the fence.

6. Mill the other end of the shelf ledge.

7. Set the shelf ledge in place. If necessary, make adjustments, before proceeding with the other three pieces.

8. Glue the shelf-ledge in place with yellow glue. Start with any piece. Spread glue on the shelf ledge rabbet and overlap recesses. Clamp the shelf ledge in place.

9. Wait until the glue has set up before you remove the clamps, then continue gluing on the remaining shelf ledges.

Rabbeting the tool tray

PAUL: While you are waiting for the glue to set on the shelf ledge, rabbet the tool tray. Here, rabbet the edge of the back piece, which will then be glued to the bottom of the tray.

1. The dado blade height is ³/₈ in. and the rabbet width is ³/₄ in., the same as the shelf-ledge rabbet.

2. Use the dado blade auxiliary fence; adjust it right next to the blades.

3. Rabbet the edge of the back of the tool tray.

4. Glue the back to the tool tray bottom. We are getting close to finishing. Don't despair.

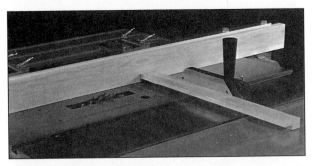

When milling the leg recess in the shelf ledge, the rip fence acts as a stop.

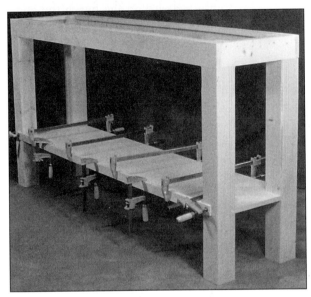

Glue the shelf ledge to the shelf. Alternate the clamps across the width of the shelf to draw the pieces together, and also clamp from the top to the bottom of the shelf.

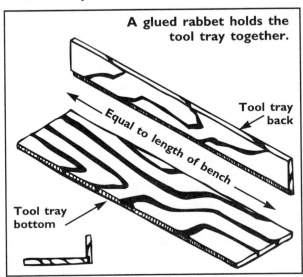

A glued rabbet holds the tool tray together.

Tool tray back

Equal to length of bench

Tool tray bottom

Put the leg frame and vise on the bench top and clamp the tool tray in place.

Use your combination square to transfer the vise stop measurement down the length of the bench.

Preassembling the Bench

PAM: Before you attach anything, determine the edge of the bench that will hold your vise. This will give you the bench-dog stop placement, which can affect where the frame is attached. With me? Keep going.

1. Put the bench top on the sawhorses with the good face up. Figure out which edge is the front.

2. Figure out where you want your vise. I placed my vise on the right end of the bench as I face the front edge. Place a big X on the table at whichever corner you choose.

3. Flip the bench top over so the good face is down.

4. Transfer the X mark for the vise to the bottom side of the bench top.

5. Place the vise, upside down, over the X mark, and make sure it's flush against the bench corners.

6. Push up the stop (that metal bar that pops out of the top). With your combination square, measure from the outside edge of the vise to the outside edge of the stop.

7. Transfer that measurement down the length of the benchtop.

8. Reset the combination square to measure from the outside edge of the vise to the inside edge of the stop. Run this measurement down the length of the bench top. You should have two parallel lines running down the length of the bench top. These are the perimeters for the bench dogs holes. When you go to place the frame on the bench, you have to position the apron outside of the bench dog hole perimeters. If you didn't do this, and you randomly drilled for the bench dog stops, you could

run into the apron and make a real mess of it. Drilling though a cleat is fine, but not the apron.

9. Place the frame on the bench. Give the frame a couple of inches clearance from the bench vise rails.

10. Depending on how wide the top is, position the cleat on the frame over the bench dog perimeter lines; this positioning allows for drilling through the cleat for a bench stop, but there should be enough room here so you don't run into the apron. If your bench top is wide, you can place the frame as far away from the bench dog marks as you want, but make sure there is enough room on the other side to attach the tool tray.

11. Set the tool tray in place. Use clamps at both ends, since this piece will want to fall off. The bottom should overlap no less than 3 in. The tray can rest flush against the apron, or it can be set away from it.

12. At the edge of the tray, run a pencil line down the length of the bench. You will need this indexing mark to position the tray when you glue it. However, if your tray rests against the apron, the apron will be your index.

Don't continue until you are satisfied with the position of each piece.

Fasten the Frame, Tool Tray, and Vise

PAM: Don't just start aimlessly screwing things together. If the cleat is placed on the outside bench dog stop mark, then you will need to mark the front edge of the bench for the bench dog stops. If both the fasteners and the bench dog stops are in the cleats, you need to position

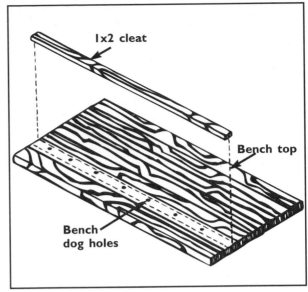

Lay out the bench dog holes and position the cleat on the top. Make sure the cleat won't interfere with the apron. Don't drill the holes yet.

Put the tool tray in position and mark the glue perimeter.

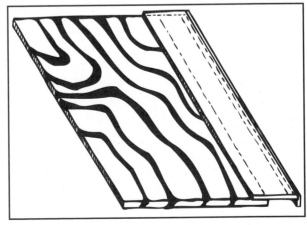

them so they don't run into each other. Otherwise, you might drill a bench dog stop and hit a screw, which will ruin your bit—and your day.

Bench-dog placement

1. Determine the opening capacity of your vise. The instructions should tell you. If they don't, then open the vise all the way and measure the inside distance. Whatever that measurement is, subtract 1 in. My vise opens to 9 in., so I set my bench dog stop holes every 8 in. Set yours accordingly; this isn't an exact science. Use a story pole marked for length, or cut a scrap piece of lumber to length. Mark down the length at the edge. Later you will transfer these marks over the edge to the top of the bench.

Fastening the frame to the top

PAM: Use wood screws that are at least twice the thickness of the board you are attaching to the bench, in this case, the cleat. Since the cleat is $^3/_4$ in., use 1-$^1/_2$-in. screws. Though you can go a bit longer, don't get screws so long they go through the bench top.

Before inserting the screws, drill a pilot hole for each so you don't split the wood. Select a drill bit that is the size of the root diameter of your screw. If you have forgotten how, review Chapter 6.

1. Eyeball the bench stop marks, and between them drill pilot holes through the front cleat and into the bench top.

2. Fasten the cleat to the top with wood screws.

3. Spaced about every 8 in. or so, drill pilot holes through the remaining three cleats. Fasten with wood screws.

Attaching the tool tray

PAM: Unless you have deep-jawed clamps, you can't clamp the tool tray properly for glue to adhere to both the tray and bench top. Here the screws are going to act as clamps.

Before you remove the tray to spread glue on it, you need to mark a line for the glue perimeters. Get under the bench, and mark a line on the tool tray bottom where it meets the bench top.

1. Remove the tool tray. Spread the glue between the outside edge and the pencil mark. I use polyurethane glue since this is a rather large area to cover.

2. Place the tool tray back on the bench. Position it against the apron, or on the indexing mark. Clamp at both ends.

3. Drill pilot holes about every 9 to 10 in.

4. Fasten with wood screws. The screws act like mini-clamps; you can remove them after the glue sets if you like.

The vise and vise extension

PAM: For the vise dog to function properly, the vise cannot extend above the bench top. It can sit a bit below the bench top, but no more than ¹/₈ in.

1. Take the vise apart, if you can, and set the rails aside. Pay attention to how you do this. For the vise to work properly, it has to be put back together the same way it came apart.

2. Set the inside of the vise upside down on the bench and mark around the vise. To set the vise flush with the bench top, you will have to use shims. Look around the shop for scrap wood, you should have plenty of that by now. I found that a 2x4 was just about the right depth, yet it wasn't wide enough. So I edge-glued two 2x4 scraps together, then trimmed them to length.

To find the size of the vise extension, set the vise in position, remove its rails, and mark around it.

Build up and shim the vise extension until the top of the vise is flush with the bench top. Rabbet the extension so the vise fits flush against the edge of the bench.

When I finally mounted the vise, I still had to use shims to get the height right. You have to tinker with this, using lumber around the shop and building it up.

3. Stack and glue wood until you reach the correct depth for the vise extension.

4. Trim the extension to size. Depending on which way the grain is going, either rip or crosscut it.

5. Set the vise on top of the extension and look at the bottom corner of the vise. As you can see, it isn't square, but round. You need to mill the wood so the vise fits flush against the extension, otherwise you won't be able to attach the vise to the extension correctly.

There are a few options as to how to get the vise extension to fit. You can rabbet the recess with dado blades; you can use a round-over bit with your router; or you can make repeated passes with the combination blade on the saw until the required rabbet width and depth is reached. (It doesn't take much, just a few passes of the blade.) I used the last option, which worked fine.

6. Place the vise and extension block on the bench. Check underneath the bench to make sure the vise is flush with the top, or just a little bit below the edge.

7. Remove the vise. Glue the extension block to the bench.

8. When the glue has set up, fasten the vise to the extension block.

9. Turn the bench upright!

Tool-tray ends and bench dogs

1. Install the tool tray ends. This isn't fancy work; look around the shop for scrap wood. You don't need the tray ends to extend above the benchtop. A 1x2 cut to size and glued in works fine.

2. Make the bench dogs. These are stops on top of the bench that are used to brace wood against the vise dog. Use dowels; they are cheap, can easily be replaced, and won't ruin a tool that is run into them. If you just stick a dowel down the bench dog hole, it will probably fall through, so you need to put caps on the dowels. You will need a piece of 1x2 about 12 in. long—cut up a story pole.

3. Measure for the cap length (1-$\frac{1}{2}$ to 2 in. is fine). Mark for cap length, side by side down the lumber; three is plenty, but make more if you're up to it—six would be excessive, you only use them one at a time. If you are using $\frac{1}{2}$-in. dowels, you will use a $\frac{1}{2}$-in. drill bit for the cap holes.

4. Clamp down the cap lumber. Find the center of each cap, and drill the holes for the dowels. Don't go all the way though the wood—there won't be anything for the glue to hang onto. Drill into the wood about half the thickness of the lumber.

5. Cut the caps to length with a handsaw.

6. Cut the dowels to length. Bench top thickness plus a 1-in. underhang plus the cap recess equals the dowel length. You want the dowel to go all the way through the bench and extend about an inch on the other side. You are doing this in case the bench dog gets stuck. Then you can take a mallet and tap the end back up though the bench. Waxing your dowels will also help prevent them from getting stuck.

7. Spread glue into the cap recess. Insert a dowel and clamp.

Bench dog stops/placement

PAM: The bench dog stops line up down the bench with the vise stop, so you'll need a reference mark for this position.

Make bench dogs from dowels and caps of 1x2.

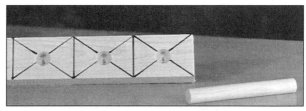

Mark the caps on a piece of 1x2. Locate and drill holes for the dowels, then cut off each cap.

Glue and clamp the dowel and cap assembly.

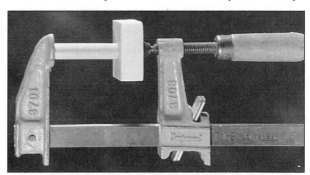

1. Set the combination square against the outside edge of the vise and measure to the center of the vise stop.

2. Transfer the measurement down the length of the bench.

3. If you've already marked the edge of the bench top in reference to the fasteners, transfer those marks across the top. You will also want to mark where the legs are. You don't want to drill a stop down them; transfer the leg placement across the bench top. If your bench dog hole falls into the leg area, readjust the hole.

4. Using the same drill-bit size as the dowel circumference ($1/2$ in.), drill all the way through the bench at each bench stop mark.

The last thing

PAM: You will want to add wood faces to the vise jaws. If you don't, the metal jaws will mar the wood. Use baltic birch cut to the size of the jaws. Fasten the baltic birch to the jaw face using machine screws the size of the holes that are in the jaw faces for this purpose. Naturally, countersink the holes.

Finishing

PAM: There is nothing fast about finishing; a good finish takes a fairly long time to produce. However, this is a workbench, a tool you will use, not something you are going to display in a museum. And the real problem here is that you are probably sick of the bench. I sure was when I finished mine. I would have left it unfinished, but that's not the craftsman way. Finishing is a science in itself and it's hard to guess what you might be after. But I bet you're looking for something fast. You need to analyze the situation. Break the bench into two categories: the top and the frame. The bench top will get the most use; therefore, it should get the most protection. In theory, what you use on the bench top, you should use on the frame, but that's a technicality I overlooked.

Review the material on sanding then sand everything. Round over all sharp edges with sandpaper by hand: Don't use a power sander for rounding over because it will take off way too much wood.

As you get into finer lumber and more intricate projects, finishing will become very important to you. Meanwhile, our main objective is understanding how wood is milled into pieces that fit together, and then joined so that they stay together.

8 THE ROUTER TABLE

This router table features a plastic laminate top, jointer fence, dust-collection hood, finger guard, and leg-mounted safety switch.

PAM: A whole new world unfolds when you have a router table. Hand-held routing is fine, and in certain cases, it's the only way to do the job. But there is nothing fun about trying to rout a small or thin strip of lumber.

With a router table, you don't have to worry about clamping down lumber, since both hands are free to control the wood. Because the router table adds weight and stability, you can use really big bits (which could be frightening in a hand-held router), and you can safely use any part of a big multi-profile bit. In addition, you can use the router table to duplicate patterns and to create all kinds of joints and decorative cuts. Finally, when you use the router table in conjunction with a jointer fence and spiral bit, you can produce the straight edges on boards that are critical to square, accurate construction. Up until now jointing hasn't really been a concern, but as you head into working with hardwoods, it will be.

Another thing: While hand-held routing creates an amazing amount of dust, router-table routing is virtually dust-free when you connect a dust-hood attachment on the router-table fence to the dust-collection system. This alone should inspire you to make this table—it did me.

The part I didn't count on, and couldn't have known until I built the table, was how much time my router table would save me in production. Before I had a router table, if I needed to make a rabbet cut I would have to rip the board to width, change to dado blades, set up the auxiliary dado fence, mill the rabbet, and on and on and on. And if I made a mistake somewhere, I'd have to backtrack, changing blades and repeating the procedures all over again. This isn't to say that you are going to throw away your dado blades—never. It just means that the router table is an invaluable tool.

Before You Begin

PAUL: We tackle this project in three parts: the table top and insert, the frame, and the fence. The table top and frame are built independently of one another and fastened together with cleats and wood screws. This section briefly introduces the parts, and gives the supplies you'll need for the project.

What you need to buy (or order)

PAUL: If you have trouble finding any of the items on this list, consult a woodworker's store or catalog

The router-table top. Go buy one. After Pam and I built two router-table tops out of plastic laminate, we decided that for the expense and time involved, having a top made would have been the way to go. All home centers have kitchen and bath sections, and most lumberyards can special-order custom countertops. A router table top would be considered a modified countertop. Another source are the woodworking catalogs (but they are more expensive).

How big do you want your router table to be? Mine measures 24 in. by 36 in.; I wouldn't go any smaller than this. If you want the hole in the middle cut out for the insert (described next) be aware that this will add considerably to the cost of the top; you will need to know the size of the plastic insert before you order the top.

Plastic insert: This is a piece of plastic that is attached to the router base. The router and insert are inverted and set into the router table. Usually offered with the insert are three flathead machine bolts at least ³/₄ in. long, which attach the router base to the insert—make sure to order these.

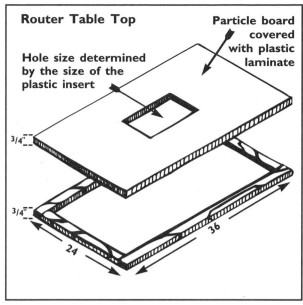

Here's how a custom fabricator will build a router table top. The finished edge thickness is 1-¹/₂".

Router-fence finger guard: This item gives you a visual and physical reference to the location of the bit.

Router-table dust-hood attachment: This is essential for dust-free routing.

Extra router base: While optional, this gizmo will let you attach one base to the insert and leave it there.

Router-fence safety switch. This essential item is basically a modified extension cord. The switch mounts on a table leg, so you don't have to fumble around for the router switch.

Fence materials and hardware: Rummage around at your local hardware store (or home center) for these items.

- One piece of $3/4$-in. thick particleboard or fiberboard, 11 in. wide by 42 in. long.

- A $1/4$-in.-20 carriage bolt for the fence micro-adjustment ($1/4$ in. refers to the diameter of the bolt, 20 means how many threads per inch).

- Two washers, two nuts, and one knob (handle) to fit the carriage bolt, also for the fence's micro-adjustment.

- Threaded inserts, about ten of them. Because particleboard and fiberboard don't hold fasteners well, the threaded inserts ensure you will always have something to fasten to. Purchase threaded inserts that are compatible with your screw and knob sizes.

- A $1/4$-in. medium-duty setting tool for the fence pivot. A setting tool is a steel rod used to set wall anchors. Although the package says "$1/4$ in.," the diameter of the rod is $1/2$ in. Ignore the setting pin at the top; these come knurled (rough all over) or smooth—you want smooth. Otherwise, if you can find it, you can make a pivot out of $1/2$-in. dia. steel rod, cut to about 4 in. long.

- A piece of $3/4$-in. thick polypropylene, a slick white plastic that bolts to the front face of the jointer fence. Measure the fence for height and length, and add 4 in. to the length. Some woodworking catalogs and crafts stores carry this material.

- Six to eight 2¾-in. long flat head machine bolts to attach the polypropylene to the fence. You'll also need 12 to 16 washers (two per bolt), and 6 to 8 nuts for the bolts. Buy 5 or 6 fender washers to shim the outfeed part of the jointer fence; the fender washers are set between the polypropylene and particleboard or fiberboard.

For cutting the insert hole:

- Router with a ½-in. flush-trim bit, preferably with a ½-in. shank.

- Drill and brad point bits.

- Handful of 1¼ in. wood or drywall screws, to fasten the flush-trim fence to the table top.

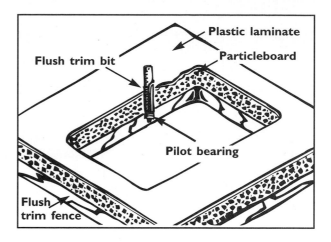

Jigsaw the hole for the router base, then clean up the hole by routing with a flush-trim bit. The bit's pilot bearing rides on a fence attached to the bottom of the router table top.

Installing the Insert in the Table Top

PAM: Got the top? Good. If you had the router insert hole cut for you, then proceed to the cleats (the shelf the router insert is attached to.) But if you're staring at a smooth surface, you need to cut the insert hole.

Cutting the insert hole

PAUL: For this part of the process, you need a flush-trim bit. This bit does just what it says—it trims edges flush. If you look at your bit you will notice that it has a bearing on the bottom; this bearing rides on the edge of a fence that rests below the work being trimmed. Obviously, any deviation in the fence will transfer to the area being routed.

1. Turn your table top over, so the bottom is up and the plastic laminate faces down.

Plant the plastic insert in the center of the bottom of the router table, and fit the flush trim fence around it.

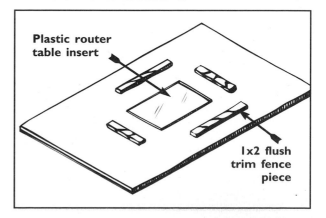

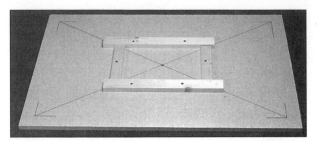

Here the 1x2 flush-trim fence has been screwed to the bottom of the router table; the plastic insert has been removed.

When jigsawing out the insert hole, get as close to the edge of the flush-trim fence as possible, but try not to ding the fence, which would make it hard to trim the opening with the flush-trim router bit.

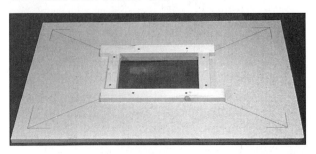

Center the router insert on the table top. (If you have forgotten how to find the center of things, refer to chapter 6, where we center the levelers in the workbench legs.)

2. Build the flush trim fence around the router insert. I use 1x2 lumber for the fence, but anything straight will do. Until you get the first two parts of the fence in place, everything will want to slide around, so go slow and keep readjusting.

3. Cut the fence sides first. It doesn't matter if they extend beyond the plastic insert.

4. Place one side against the insert. Pre-drill the fastener holes, then fasten the fence to the top using three wood screws.

5. Set the other fence side against the opposite side of the insert. Again, pre-drill the fastener holes, then fasten the fence using three wood screws.

6. Mark an end piece to fit tightly between the side fences.

7. Crosscut the end piece to length. Repeat for the other end.

8. Pre-drill and then fasten the ends in place with two wood screws, using the plastic insert as an index.

9. Remove the plastic insert. If it is trapped by the flush-trim fence, remove one of the fence ends, lift out the insert, then refasten the end.

10. With a jigsaw, remove most of the waste (you will clean up the hole with the flush-trim bit). To start drill a $1/2$-in. hole through the table and insert the jigsaw blade in the hole then start the saw.

11. Saw out the section framed by the flush-trim fence, leaving no more than $1/8$ in. of wood to trim-rout.

12. Clean up the edges using a router and the flush-trim bit. Turn the table top over so the flush trim fence is underneath. Adjust the bit so that the bearing is riding on the fence below the top. Make repeated passes at the particleboard until the bearing is riding smoothly on the fence under the table.

Which way to rout? A router bit spins clockwise. You want to feed the wood into the bit. If you are working on the outside of a piece, rout counterclockwise. If you are routing the inside of a piece, then rout clockwise. Use the diagram as a reference for which way to go.

13. When the insert edge has been routed, turn the table over and remove the flush-trim fence.

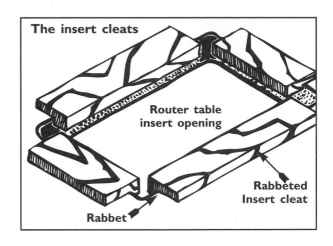

Making the Insert Cleats

PAM: The cleats support the insert. A loose insert means a loose router, with its bit flying around at 22,000 RPM while you are trying to feed wood into it—a nasty thought. Also, the cleats hold the leveling screws. You need the insert to fit flush with the table top; too high, and you will have problems starting and finishing the cut; too low, and you'll have the same problem. We'll show you how to add leveling screws later on.

For the cleats, pine is fine. Make them from a board large enough to comfortably mill on the table saw; after you mill the rabbets, crosscut the cleats to length. I used 1x4 lumber and then later ripped it to width; a 1x2 didn't seem wide enough, but a 1x4 seemed like overkill.

1. Turn the router table top so that the bottom is facing up. It's vital that you have the table top on a flat surface; any variation in the surface will alter the insert depth. Drop the insert into the hole.

2. Set a small piece of scrap lumber on top of the insert. Mark the edge of the scrap

Set the plastic insert in the hole, then place a small piece of scrap on top of the insert. Mark the thickness of the table top on the scrap.

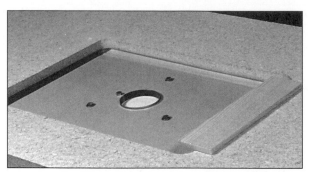

Test-fit the router cleat to the table top, keeping the insert in position.

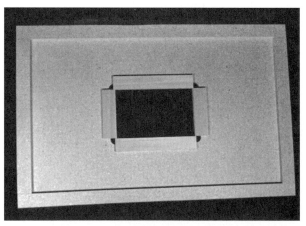

Here the insert cleats are in place on the bottom of the router table top.

where it meets the bottom table surface. You are going to remove the lumber between the plastic insert and the mark when you rabbet the cleats. Make a big X on the top surface of the scrap so you will know which side is facing up.

3. Stack your dado blades to any width. (I use a ³/₄-in. width.) Attach your auxiliary dado fence to your table-saw fence. Adjust the blade height for the rabbet: Place the scrap lumber next to the dado blades with the big X facing up. Adjust the blades until they are just below the pencil mark. Remember, remove everything but the pencil line.

4. Since you can't safely test-rabbet the small scrap used to transfer the insert cleat depth, use a longer board. Mill a ³/₄-in. rabbet along the edge of the board.

5. Test-fit the rabbeted cleat, cutting off length if necessary. If the cleat doesn't quite reach the insert, raise the dado blades and remove more wood. (If the rabbet is too deep, mill a new test piece.) Don't rabbet the cleats until you have the rabbet depth correct.

6. Rabbet the lumber for the cleats from 1x4 lumber; the wider the rabbet, the more gluing surface you'll have—I ran my rabbets at a little over an inch. Mill a rabbet down the length of the board, then adjust the fence away from the blades to widen the rabbet. Make sure you rabbet enough lumber for all four cleats.

7. Now change your sawblade and rip the cleat to about 3 in. wide. The solid part of the wood (not the rabbeted edge) should be at least ³/₄ to 1 in. wide to hold the fasteners.

8. Set the cleat on the table next to the insert hole and mark it for length. Crosscut the

cleat to length. Make sure it fits in the insert hole before crosscutting the remaining cleats. The cleats don't have to fit tightly—close enough will do. Crosscut the next length, and then fit the ends in between the lengths.

9. Remove the plastic insert. Glue the cleats on one by one. Spread glue on the surface of the rabbet that rests underneath the table. Clamp the rabbet to the table bottom. That's all for now—the router insert gets fastened to the cleats later on.

Making the Frame

PAUL: The frame is built very much like the workbench frame, except it doesn't have a shelf. Believe me, you don't want a shelf underneath—all it does is catch sawdust and block your feet when you want to stand close. As with the workbench, the size of the table top determines all other measurements.

PAM: Take a minute to look carefully at your workbench. Do you see all the little gaps between the 2x4s? (Look past the glue.) Do you see any gaps in the rabbets and dadoes? Of course you do—I'd be surprised if you didn't. But in this chapter, it's time to start tightening everything up, to start to understand the meaning of "square" and "true." The ability to square boards and mill perfect joints comes only with practice. Paul can automatically mill a joint so that it fits perfectly. Me? Well, I still have little gaps here and there; I haven't been at this as long as Paul. It can be discouraging, frustrating work, trying to mill a faultless piece, but people learn from their mistakes. And with beginners, there will always be mistakes. I have found that while mistakes that compromise the structural integrity of the piece must be corrected, with the little mistakes, you can often just keep on going. Remember, this is a piece of shop furniture.

Two rails and a stretcher stabilize the outer table frame. It's built much like the workbench in Chapter 7.

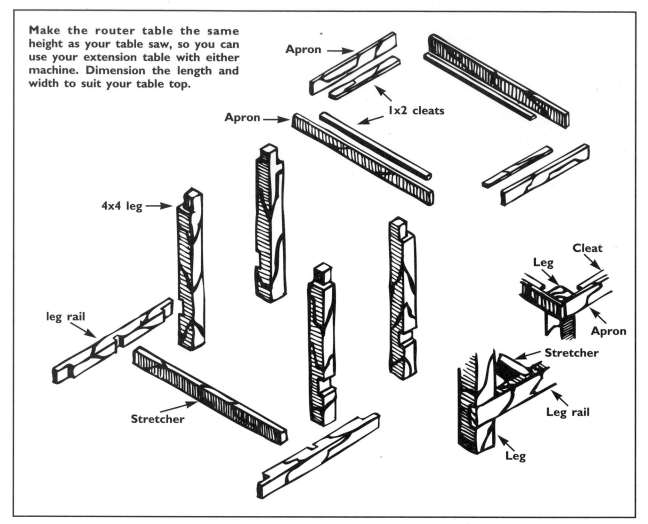

Make the router table the same height as your table saw, so you can use your extension table with either machine. Dimension the length and width to suit your table top.

Apron

1x2 cleats

Apron

4x4 leg

leg rail

Stretcher

Cleat

Leg

Apron

Stretcher

Leg rail

Leg

The frame is the easy part of this project, even though it's more finely fitted than that of the bench. The frame involves lap joints, which aren't difficult, but need to be milled correctly to get enough gluing surface as well as to look nice. Start with the legs, and be sure to cut one extra leg and rail. When you start fine-tuning a cut, mill the extra piece first; if you make an error, it won't be on the actual legs

Roughing out the lumber dimensions

PAM: As with the workbench, the frame dimensions are determined by the router table top.

The legs—4x4 pine, five pieces (the extra one is used to transfer measurements).

Shoot to have your router table match the height of your table saw. That way you can use your extension tables with both.

The apron—1x4 pine, two ends (the same width as the table top)and two sides (the same length as the table top).

The cleats—1x2 pine, four pieces. The ends and sides match the length of the apron ends and sides.

The leg rails—2x4 pine, three pieces (the extra one is used to set rabbet and dado dimensions). The length of the leg rail equals the width of the table top.

The stretcher—2x4 pine, one piece. The stretcher is as long as the table top.

Extras—You'll need two or three extra 1x2x8 pieces of pine for story poles if you don't have them already.

Making the apron

1. Start with determining the length of the apron sides. If you have table ledges, place a story pole against an inside ledge and mark the pole at the opposite ledge. Don't make the apron fit so tightly inside the ledges that you can't comfortably remove the pieces. If you don't have ledges, measure so that the apron fits about 2 in. in from all edges; record this length on a story pole.

2. Transfer the apron length mark to the apron lumber, and crosscut the apron side to length. Check the dimension before you cut the second apron side. Set up a stop block, and use the first apron to transfer the measurement. Mill the second apron side.

3. Mark the ends. Set the apron sides in place on the table, and transfer the inside width measurement to a story pole.

4. Crosscut the first apron end; check its size before you mill the next apron end. Set up a stop block and mill the second apron end.

5. Dry-fit and clamp the apron pieces in place.

Constructing the legs

PAM: Leave the apron dry-clamped in place on the table; as you go along, keep clamping in the new piece (legs, leg rails, stretcher), to help keep you oriented.

1. Crosscut the legs to height. Use the same method as with the workbench legs.

2. Cut an extra leg to use as scrap. Clamp the legs into place on the table bottom.

The apron, made from 1x4 pine, sits about 2 in. away from the edges of the table top. If your top has ledges, build the apron inside the ledges—aim for a snug fit without forcing.

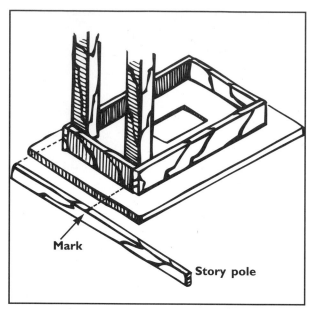

Mark

Story pole

Mark the length of the rails on a story pole. The rail should be as long as the outside width of the apron.

Leg rails

PAM: Note that the leg rails and apron ends are not the same size. The leg rails run the entire width of the apron, not the width minus an apron end thickness.

If you don't square the 2x4s, the lap joints will have fairly large gaps. There's not much you can do about squaring the 4x4 legs; the edges will have to remain eased. But squaring the rail and stretcher lumber will give a cleaner joint.

1. Rip the eased edge from each 2 x 4, just as you did for the workbench top.

2. Measure for the rails. Place the story pole across the entire width of the apron end and mark the pole. Transfer the measurement to the rail. Crosscut the rail to size. Check the rail for accuracy; set it against the apron width.

4. Set up a stop block, using the first rail as a reference. Crosscut the next rail to size.

6. Crosscut an extra rail for setting measurements. Square the stretcher lumber, but don't cut the stretcher yet. It's the last thing you cut, after all the pieces have been glued together.

Rabbeting the legs for the apron

PAM: The top of each leg is rabbeted to accept the apron (the same as the workbench). To get through this quickly, use a dado blade width of ³/₄ in. And remember, with dado blades you are milling a lot of wood, so push the work through the blades slowly. If you hear a lot of noise, you're going too fast.

1. Use the extra leg to fine-tune this cut before you mill the rest of the legs. This is exactly what you did for the workbench aprons, so refer to the "Rabbeting the legs for the apron" section in Chapter 7 for the rabbet width and dado blade height; also review using the fence as a stop block.

Come back here to mill the rabbet, because we have to fine-tune the cut.

2. Before you mill the entire rabbet, test the dado blade for the correct depth. Make one pass on the top edge of the extra leg. You don't have to mill the entire width of the apron rabbet—this is just a test.

3. Set the apron into the rabbet. Are the surfaces flush? If the apron is above the leg, raise the dado blades. If the apron rests below the leg surface, lower the dado blades. You can turn the leg over and use the other side. Mill the leg until you have the correct dado blade height.

4. Still using the extra leg, mill the rabbet width. Start the rabbet at the top of the leg and work your way down until you are close to the pencil mark; then stop.

5. Set the fence as a stop against the top of the leg. From here on, you are going to nibble away at the rabbet, removing $1/16$ in., or less. After each cut, set the apron in the rabbet. Getting close? Keep milling the rabbet by fractions and moving the fence, until you have the exact width for the rabbet.

When the width is exact, you're ready to mill the apron rabbets on the legs. Since the width is set, it doesn't matter if you start with the leg against the fence or work your way toward the fence. There are two apron rabbets on each leg. Put an X on the legs for rabbet placement. It's easy to mill a rabbet on the wrong side.

6. Mill two apron rabbets on each leg.

7. Dry-fit and clamp the apron and legs in place inside the bottom of the router table.

Making the rails

PAM: The rails join to the legs with lap joints. Lap joints are made by cutting corresponding

A lap joint increases the gluing surface while making a neat appearance.

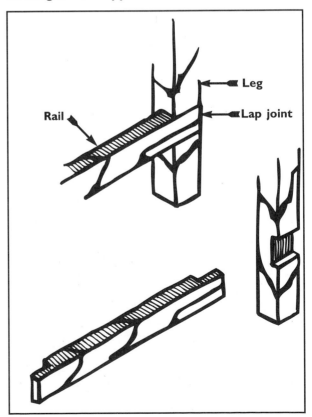

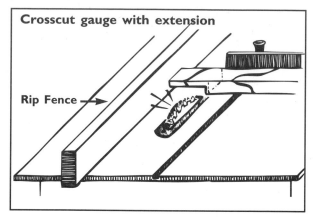

Crosscut gauge with extension

Rip Fence →

As you approach the rabbet width mark on the rail, bring the fence over and use it as a stop. Mill a fraction, check the fit, and mill some more.

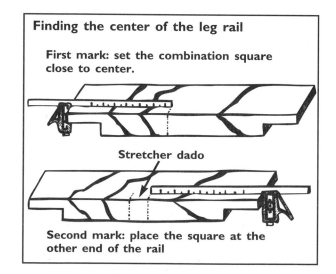

Finding the center of the leg rail

First mark: set the combination square close to center.

Stretcher dado

Second mark: place the square at the other end of the rail

recesses out of two pieces of wood. When the two pieces are glued in place, all exposed surfaces are flush, creating a smooth joint. The increased gluing surface adds strength to the joint.

You begin a lap joint by removing about half the thickness from one of the members. You then remove a corresponding amount of wood from the second member.

1. First establish the rabbet depth in the rail. Use the extra rail. Lay it next to the blades and adjust blade height to about half the rail thickness.

2. Establish the rabbet width, using the extra rail; place the rail flush against the outside of the leg, and mark the rail at the inside edge of the leg.

3. Again, the width mark is just for reference to let you know you're getting close to finishing the cut. Mill the rabbet at the outside edge of the rail and work your way toward the mark. When you get close, use the fence as a stop and mill off only fractions at a time; check the rabbet repeatedly with the leg until the correct rabbet width is obtained, that is, when the rail is flush with the outside edge of the leg.

4. Before you rabbet the rails for the lap joints, mark an X on each rail for rabbet positions. It's just for reference so you won't get confused while rabbeting.

5. Mill a rabbet on both ends of each rail. We will cut the leg laps for the rails later. Right now, since we are working on the rails, cut the dado for the stretcher.

Cutting the stretcher dado in the rails

PAM: Stick with the same dado blade height as for the rail rabbets. The stretcher dado is milled on the same side as the rail rabbets. To find the center of the rail, we use a transfer-of-measurement technique.

1. Use your scrap rail to find the center of the rail. Place your combination square at the end of the rail and set the rule at approximately the center; mark the rail. Switch to the opposite end of the rail and again mark for the center. It doesn't matter if the marks don't reach the center, or even overlap. What you should have are two marks of equal distance close to the center. It's much easier finding the center of something if the marks are close together. Label each end as shown in the drawing; this will help keep you oriented as to which end is against the fence.

2. Eyeball the center between the two marks. Center the marks on the rail (or close to it), with the dado blades. Use the fence as a stop. Note that to support this small piece of lumber, you will have to hold the board on both sides. You can do this since you aren't cutting all the way through the wood. However, you have to be very careful where you place your hands and fingers. This is a blind cut and you don't want your fingers near the blades. To help support the work, move the miter-gauge extension close to, but not touching, the fence.

3. With the first end against the fence, dado the rail.

4. Turn the rail end-for-end, so that the second end is against the fence. Mill another dado. The dado is now dead center in the board.

5. Set the edge of the stretcher lumber on the rail— how far off are you from the final dimension? Move the fence away from the blade just a little bit. Every time you do this, the dimension is doubled; to keep the rail dado centered, you have to make two passes—one cut, and then turn the board end-for-end and make the second cut.

When finding the center of the dado in the leg rail, keep your hands and fingers away from the dado blade.

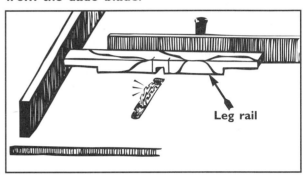

To center the dado, align the blade between the two marks. Move the fence over as a stop. Mill the dado, turn the rail end-for-end, and mill again.

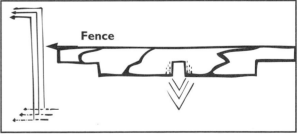

Be careful when you adjust the fence. Every change is doubled, because you have to make two cuts to keep the dado centered.

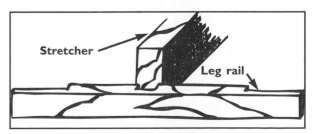

Measure dado against stretcher

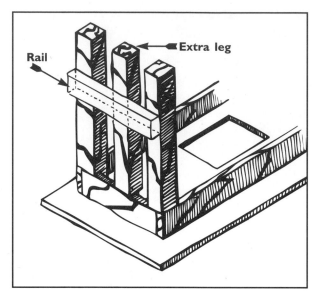

Use the extra leg to transfer the rail width to both sides of the frame.

Set the dado blade height for the second part of the lap joint. The wood that is left on the rabbet is the part that is measured for height.

6. Keep checking the stretcher lumber with the rail, and moving the fence over, by fractions, until the stretcher lumber fits the rail dado. You want it snug, but not so snug that the stretcher has to be forced into the dado. If you force the stretcher, when you go to glue it, the wood will split. If you accidentally cut the dado too large, flip the rail over, adjust the fence, and mill another stretcher dado. Work at this until you have the correct dado width for the stretcher.

7. When the stretcher width is exact, mill the stretcher dado on the rails. Note that on the rail, all dadoes are on the same side. Set a rail into place against the fence, and dado one end. Be sure not to move the fence out of position. Turn the rail end-for-end and mill the other side of the dado. Clean out the excess wood in the center of the dado.

8. Mill the remaining rail dado; repeat step.

The rail placement

PAM: The apron and legs should be dry-clamped together inside the router table; this just helps you get an idea of how high you want the rails off the floor when the frame is upright. However, use your extra leg to mark and set the blade height and dado width. Here, just place the extra leg next to one of the legs on the table.

1. Set the rail against the leg; the rail should be about a foot from the bottom of the leg. Mark on both sides of the rail to transfer the rail width to the extra leg. This is just a rough mark. It gives you a place to begin.

2. Set the dado blade height for the lap joint. The wood that is left on the rail rabbet is the part measured for the dado blade height. Place a rail rabbet next to the dado blades with the rabbeted part facing up. Set the blade height level with the remaining rabbet lumber.

3. Use the extra leg to test the dado blade for the lap depth. On the top edge of the extra leg, mill a rabbet. You have only to mill the edge—this is just to check for the correct depth.

4. Set the rail rabbet into the leg rabbet. Are the surfaces flush? If not, adjust the blades accordingly, as you did when rabbeting the legs for the apron.

   When the leg and rail surfaces are flush, you are ready to set up the double stop for the leg dado. The fence is set at an equal distance from the bottom of the leg to where the dado starts. A stop block on the miter-gauge extension sets the distance for the top of the dado; it can be a bit confusing at first and the best way to figure it out is to make a dry run through it so you know what's going on.

5. Use the extra leg. Set the bottom mark for the rail dado at the edge of the dado blades; make sure the blades are between the dado marks.

6. Set a stop block on the miter-gauge extension, resting at the end of the leg. When you start milling, you are going away from the stop block toward the fence.

7. Start milling the leg dado for the lap joint. When you get close to the full width dado mark on the leg, set the fence as a stop. Nibble away at the dado on the leg. Make a

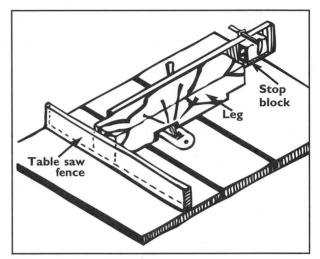

When you get close to finishing the rail dado, set the table saw fence as a stop. Move the fence over by fractions until the rail fits into the dado.

Here the rail dado is milled in the leg. Dado dimensions are set using the table-saw fence and a stop block on the miter-gauge extension.

This is how the frame should look when everything is fit together.

Use your try-square to square the leg and rail before tightening the clamp.

pass; check the width of the leg dado with the rail rabbet. Move the fence over a bit, make another pass, and so on. Do this until the rail rabbet fits snugly into the dado, creating a nice lap joint. If you have managed to oversize the dado, turn the leg over, adjust the fence, and mill a new dado. Don't dado the legs until you have it right.

9. With the legs still clamped in place inside the router table bottom, mark the legs for the rail dadoes. This is just a reference, an X on the side that is to be dadoed will do.

10. Mill the dadoes for the lap joints in the legs.

11. Fit everything together.

Gluing The Frame

PAM: Dry-clamp all the parts together. Then glue the rails into the leg dadoes, working on one leg at a time. Use your try-square to make sure everything is square. If you're feeling courageous and have enough clamps, you can glue the entire piece together all at once. (Use polyurethane glue, because it will give you time to shift pieces around before the glue sets up.)

1. Spread glue on the rail rabbet. Be sure to cover the shoulder and edges with glue. Clamp the rail into place on the leg. Use the try-square to true the leg and rail.

2. Repeat with the other rail.

3. Before you glue on the aprons, you'll need to transfer the apron length to a story pole and then clamp the pole at the length marks to the rails. This helps keep everything square. If the aprons don't quite fit, either trim the offending piece or mill a new one. Transfer the apron length dimension to a story pole. Using the length mark on the story pole, clamp across the rails, near the stretcher dadoes.

4. Spread glue on the apron/leg rabbets. Clamp the apron sides in place.

5. Set the apron ends in place, and make any adjustments. Spread glue on the leg/apron rabbets, covering all the surfaces; clamp the apron ends in place. Clamp across the width of the aprons to pull the ends in tight.

Cutting the stretcher

1. Unclamp the story pole and use it to transfer the stretcher length. Place the end of the story pole inside the rail dado. Mark the opposite end of the pole to the inside end of the other rail dado.

2. Transfer the measurement to the stretcher lumber and crosscut the stretcher to length. It's best to cut the stretcher a little long and work your way towards a tight fit.

3. Glue the stretcher in place; spread glue over the surfaces of the rail dadoes. Set the stretcher into the dadoes and place a bar clamp across the length.

The cleats

PAM: These are milled and attached the same as the workbench cleats.

What next?

PAM: After the cleats are glued on, you can finish the frame, using a finishing product of your choice, or you can continue. By the time you're done with this project, the only thing you'll want to do with the table is use it, so it's probably best to apply your finish now. You should be studying up on finishing anyway, since finishing is an art in itself. You don't have to get radical with your frame, after all, this is pine; sand it and get a couple coats of something on it, or, again, use wax.

To keep the frame stable while you are gluing on the aprons, clamp a board or story pole across the rails.

Glue and clamp the apron ends and stretcher in place. Also clamp the frame across its width to draw everything tightly together.

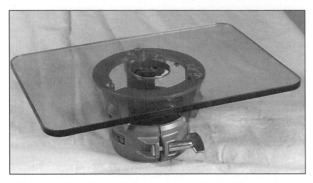

The plastic insert is attached to the router base with machine bolts.

Of Fences and Finishing Up

The jointer fence

PAUL: The fence is built from two strips of ³/₄-in. particleboard (or fiberboard, which is superior because it's smoother) face-glued together. The fence length is the same as the table-top length plus 5 in.; the fence width is 5 in., to allow room for the fingerguard in front and the dust hood in back.

Fastening the insert to the router base

PAUL: Before you make the fence, you must attach the router base to the plastic insert, set your leveling screws into the cleats, and drill the hole for the fasteners to secure the insert.

Remove the screws on the base of the router—you can't use them with the insert since they aren't long enough. If you didn't order flathead machine bolts with your insert, then take the router base screws to the hardware store and find some that are just the same, but ⁵/₈ in. long.

For this procedure, keep the router base attached to the router and put a bit in the collet; the larger the bit the better, since the bit will help you center the plastic insert hole.

1. Place the router upside down on the table. Set the insert on top of the router base. You need to look straight down over the top of the bit. The insert doesn't have to be perfectly centered, but get as close as you can.

2. Don't mark all three holes at once; and don't drill all three holes at once. Work on one hole at a time; indexing all three holes dead center is impossible. Drill one hole, realign it with the insert and base, and then mark for the next hole. Use a felt-tip marking pen, and make a dot on the insert over the center of one of the machine bolt holes.

3. Choose a brad point drill bit that will give you some clearance: The bit should be a tad

larger than the machine bolt, but definitely smaller than the head, since you have to countersink these bolts.

4. Place a sheet of white paper beneath the insert so that you can see the dot. Clamp the insert down to a scrap board. Center the drill bit right on the dot and drill the hole in the insert using short bursts of power. If you go at it all at once, you'll melt the plastic. (Plastic will burr when drilled; gently scrape off the burrs with a sharp knife.) Don't worry about countersinking the hole yet.

5. Screw the insert to the base and realign the router bit to the center of the insert.

6. Mark another dot over the next machine bolt hole and repeat the previous steps.

   If the holes aren't lining up, you'll have to use a twist bit and re-drill the hole to a larger size. This process is called chasing. Chase only one hole at a time. Realign the insert and fasten it down to see if you have to chase the next hole.

7. Once you have two holes that line up, drill the last hole. Make sure all the bolts go through the insert and thread into the holes on the router. If they don't, chase the last hole you drilled.

8. Drill countersink holes for the machine bolts. You want the head of the bolt a little bit below the insert. Be careful, don't countersink too deeply.

9. Attach the insert to the base. Thread all the bolts into the base before tightening. Don't overtighten; you want the bolts snug, but not so snug that they stress the insert.

Leveling the insert—If your insert fits perfectly flush with the table surface, skip this part and head down to securing the insert to the cleats. If your insert is above the table surface, then hand-sand the cleats until the insert is level. If

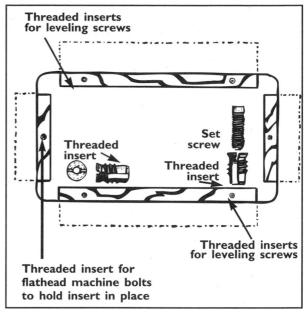

Set screws and threaded inserts retain and level the router table insert.

the insert is below the surface of the table, add threaded inserts with set screws. By raising and lowering the set screws, the router insert can be leveled flush with the table surface.

1. Use a bit that is the root diameter of the outside threads on the threaded insert. Drill a hole near each end of the side cleats (a total of four holes, as shown in the drawing).

2. Screw mating set screws flush into the threaded inserts.

Securing the insert to the cleats—Use flathead machine bolts and threaded inserts to fasten the insert to the cleats. I fasten each end of the insert; it isn't necessary to secure the sides. Go slow and make sure everything aligns perfectly.

1. Set the plastic insert in place and clamp it to the router table. Select a brad point bit the root diameter of the machine bolt you are using. Drill through the plastic and just to the ledge (this is the locating hole for the threaded insert).

2. Remove the plastic insert. Select a brad point bit that is the root diameter of the outside threads of the threaded insert. If you use a bit the same size as the threaded insert, there won't be any wood left for the outside threads to grab. Using the index mark on the cleat, drill a hole through the ledge for the threaded insert.

3. Screw the threaded insert into place on the cleat.

4. Set the plastic insert into place and lightly fasten it (with the machine bolt)—just enough to keep it from moving around.

5. Repeat the first three steps. You don't have to clamp the insert to the table since you have already fastened it at one point.

6. Remove one bolt at a time and countersink the screwholes.

Constructing the jointer fence

PAM: A jointer fence, used with a spiral bit, lets you mill straight edges on your boards. The fence has a two-part polypropylene face bolted to the particleboard, with metal shims between on the outfeed side. The shims adjust the outfeed fence to compensate for the thickness of the cut. You can also use the jointer fence as a regular fence, to guide the work, but you have to take the shims out. I got tired of re-configuring my jointer fence, so I made a regular fence to pop on and off as needed; I suggest you do the same. A regular fence doesn't have a polypropylene face, it's just two pieces of particleboard or fiberboard glued together.

1. To figure fence length, use a story pole. Measure across the length of the router table top and add about 5 in. You want enough fence to reach past the diagonal corner when the fence is centered at one edge of the table; the longer the fence, the more surface to support the board.

2. Make the fence width at least 2 in. taller than the height of your table-saw fence. If you make the router fence the same height, there won't be room for the finger guard.

3. Rip and crosscut one piece of particleboard to exact size, and one slightly larger. You do this to allow for slippage during gluing. When the glue has dried and cured, flush-trim the larger piece to match the smaller, which is the actual dimension of the fence.

4. Before you continue, check the fence for warp. If the fence has warped, and they do, forget accurate cuts. Set the fence on edge on a long piece of paper. Draw a pencil mark down the entire length of the edge.

5. Turn the fence end-for-end, and place that edge on the pencil mark. Again, mark down the entire length of the edge.

To check for a warped fence, draw a line, then reverse the fence end for end and draw another line. If the lines are parallel, the fence is straight. If the lines are cupped or bowed, make a new fence.

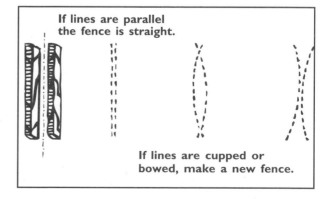

If lines are parallel the fence is straight.

If lines are cupped or bowed, make a new fence.

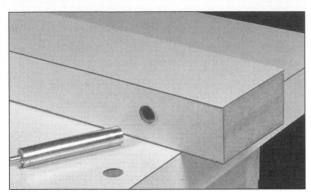

Use a setting tool for the fence and table pivot.

6. If you set the edge right on the pencil mark, there should no variance; the mark should be one straight line. If you marked the second edge close to the first line, then these lines should be parallel. If the marks overlap, or move away from each other, the fence is warped. Make a new fence.

Marking the table for the pivot position— If you have finished your frame, then secure the table top (with 1-1/4-in. wood screws) to the cleats; pre-drill and use a fastener about every 7 in. or so.

1. Center the fence over the insert and across the length of the table.

2. Mark both edges of the fence on the table. Move the fence, find the center between the marks (eyeballing this is fine), and mark the center on the top of the table. Locate the pivot hole about 1-1/2 in. from the edge.

3. Set the fence back on the table next to the pivot mark. The fence should overhang the table edge by about 2 in. This gives you something to hang onto when you are removing the fence. Transfer the pivot mark to the bottom center of the fence.

4. Get out the setting tool and check the diameter. Mine was 1/2 in. You can use a brad point to drill through the plastic laminate top, but once you drill through the very top of the laminate, you will find you can't go any farther. Stop. The laminate is making its own stop-collar at the end of the bit. Stop drilling, remove the laminate piece at the end of the bit, and then resume drilling. To figure out how far the setting tool goes into the top without going through, use a felt-tip marker and draw a line around the setting tool at about the center.

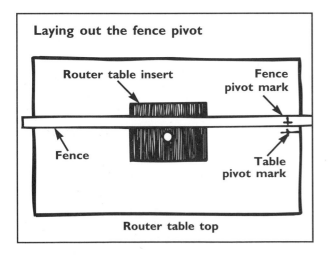

Laying out the fence pivot

Router table insert

Fence pivot mark

Fence

Table pivot mark

Router table top

6. Drill a perpendicular hole into the table—this hole must be strictly vertical. Don't go all the way through the table top. (If you do, you'll have to glue a little block as a stop underneath the table, no big deal.) Drill a little, check the setting tool to see if you're getting close to the center length of it, drill a little, check the setting tool, and so on.

7. Drill the pivot hole into the bottom of the fence. Again, keep it perpendicular.

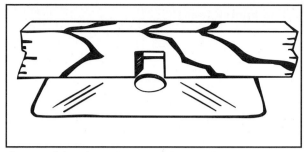

Cut a bit-clearance hole half-way up the fence.

Making the router-bit clearance on the fence— Place the setting tool in the fence, and place the fence in the pivot, and swing it back and forth a few times. Admire it. If you've made it this far, you've come a long way. Before you add the polypropylene to the face of the fence, you need to dado a bit clearance in the fence. This clearance is the size of the insert hole, and how tall the clearance is depends on your sawblades. Use an extension fence on your miter gauge, a combination blade or crosscut blade, and nibble away at the clearance hole.

1. Set the fence into its pivot on the router table; center the fence on the router insert. Mark the fence on both sides of the insert bit hole.

2. Place the router fence on the table saw, and use the table-saw fence as a stop. Set the blade height, but don't remove more than half of the fence; if you do, you'll weaken the fence considerably.

3. Mill out the bit clearance. Using a combination blade will take time, so nibble away at the fence.

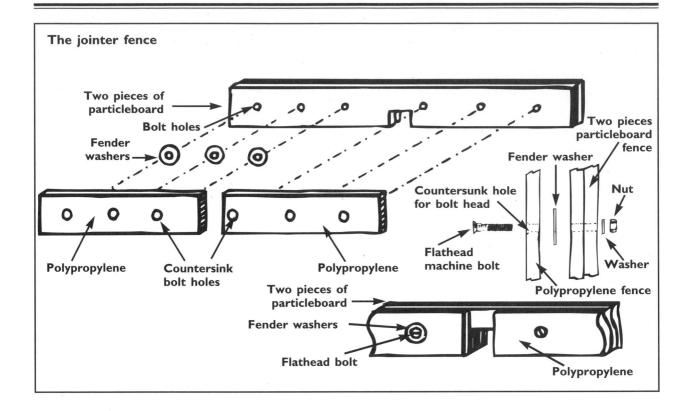

The jointer fence

Two pieces of particleboard

Bolt holes

Fender washers

Polypropylene

Countersink bolt holes

Polypropylene

Two pieces particleboard fence

Fender washer

Countersunk hole for bolt head

Flathead machine bolt

Nut

Washer

Polypropylene fence

Two pieces of particleboard

Fender washers

Flathead bolt

Polypropylene

Milling the polypropylene—Polypropylene cuts fine with combination or rip blades. It is rather slick, so be careful.

1. If you need to rip the polypropylene to the height of the fence, go ahead and do so.

2. You need to mill the polypropylene so that you end up with two pieces; one for the infeed side, the other for the outfeed side.

Position the finger guard to align over the bit clearance in the fence.

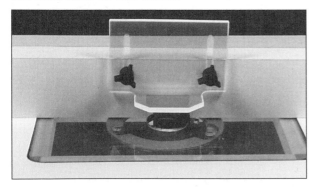

The outfeed parts can be longer, because the longer the outfeed, the more support the board will have.

3. Measure and crosscut the polypropylene to fit the router fence on both sides of the bit clearance.

4. Before you fasten the polypropylene to the fence, position and mark locating holes for the dust hood, so you won't place any bolts in these areas.

5. Leave the router fence on the table and clamp the polypropylene in place on the front of the fence.

6. Mark and drill holes for the bolts. Brad points work fine with polypropylene. I used three bolts on the infeed part of the fence and four bolts in the outfeed because it was larger. Polypropylene will clog the drill bit, so you have to keep backing it out. Countersink the bolt holes.

7. Leave the clamps on while you fasten the front of the fence in place with bolts. For the rear fence, remove the polypropylene and add a fender washer metal shim to each bolt, between the polypropylene and fence. Bolt the polypropylene to the fence.

The Finger guard

PAM: The finger guard should have its own knobs. If it doesn't, go find some at the hardware store; you also need threaded inserts to attach the knobs to the fence.

1. Align the finger guard over the fence clearance. Play around with this and see how far up the guard will go before it bottoms out on the knob holes.

2. Use the finger guard and mark the knob/hole positions for the threaded insert on the fence. There isn't much room for slop here, you want everything to line up exactly.

3. Use a drill bit that is compatible with your threaded inserts, and make sure the knobs fit the threaded inserts. If the threaded insert package says $^{11}/_{32}$ in., then use a $^{11}/_{32}$-in. drill bit. If you don't have a reference, use a bit the root diameter of the threaded insert.

4. Drill the holes. Screw the threaded insert into place. Attach the bit guard.

The dust hood

PAM: The dust hood attaches to the fence, not the table. I had to cut triangular pieces of wood that fit inside my dust hood to support the fasteners. If this procedure doesn't work for you, improvise.

1. Place the triangular dust hood edge over the corner of a 2-ft. long board.

2. Set the table-saw miter gauge to 45 degrees and cut off the corner of the board at the mark. I had to make several cuts to get the

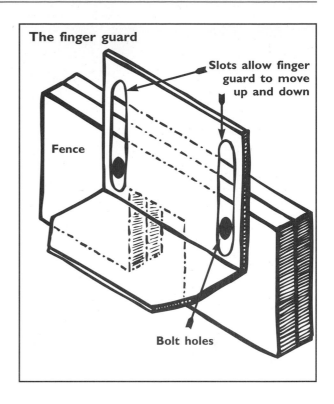

The finger guard

Slots allow finger guard to move up and down

Fence

Bolt holes

Align the dust hood to fit over the bit clearance on the back of the fence.

The micro-adjustment for the fence sits at the edge of the router table so it can be clamped down.

fit right; each time I returned the miter gauge to square and re-cut my board square before making another 45- degree cut.

3. Use double-stick carpet tape to tape the triangular pieces in place inside the dust hood.

4. You need to drill a horizontal pilot hole through the wood and into the fence. This is where it gets tricky, since you can't clamp the dust hood to the fence. You can brace and clamp a board against the bottom, and hang onto the dust hood at the top. Work on one hole at a time; fasten the hood to the fence and work on the other hole. Start the hole at an angle, and then reposition the bit so that it drills a horizontal hole.

The micro fence adjustment

PAM: You might be tempted to skip this part, but don't. Paul devised the micro-adjustment to make it possible to achieve accurate settings for joints. A micro fence adjustment does just that—it makes minute fence adjustments, and the more routing you do, the more you'll appreciate this tool. You will definitely be using a threaded insert here for the carriage bolt, so make sure they are compatible. As you build this, keep everything flush on the router table.

1. For the micro-adjustment, you need a piece of 1x2 cut to the height of the fence; this piece is called the post.

2. For the base, use a piece of 1x4 cut square. Then glue the edge grain of the 1x4 to the face grain of the 1x2. Do not glue end grain to face grain.

3. Locate the carriage bolt placement for the micro fence adjustment and router fence. At the edge of the router table, clamp the post to the router fence.

4. The hole in the post and the hole in the fence have to align exactly to accept the

The micro fence adjustment

1x2 post

Hole for carriage bolt

Edge-glue base to post

1x4 base cut square

carriage bolt. Use a brad point the thread diameter of the carriage bolt and drill (about center on the post) through the post and into the fence. (Don't go very far into the fence, you just want a locating hole.)

Duplicate this sequence of washers and nuts before you thread the nuts up the carriage bolt to secure the knob.

5. Unclamp the micro-adjustment. Drill a hole in the fence for the threaded insert; this time use a twist bit since you will be chasing (enlarging) the hole in the router fence. Use a drill bit that corresponds with the threaded insert size. And when you drill into the fence for the threaded insert, don't drill through the other side of the fence. Fasten the threaded insert into place in the fence.

6. Thread the knob, washers, and bolts onto the carriage bolt in the sequence shown in the photo. If the carriage bolt and knob don't fit together (mine didn't), you need to glue (super-glue works) the knob to the bolt; otherwise, when you go to turn the knob, it won't turn the carriage bolt. After you thread the two nuts up the carriage bolt to the post, tighten the nuts against each other; this locks the nuts together so they won't loosen when the carriage bolt is turned, and they keep the knob and washer snug against the post. However, if the knob won't move, loosen the nuts. Screw the carriage bolt into the threaded insert in the fence. You now have a fence that will make hair-line adjustments.

7. Here's how to use the micro-adjustment: After the router fence has been aligned with the bit, run a piece of scrap through the bit. If minute adjustments are necessary to achieve the desired cut, clamp the micro-adjusting fence base to the table; turn the carriage bolt either way to make subtle fence adjustments.

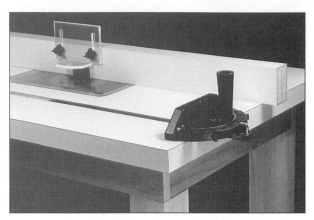

You can use your table-saw miter gauge in a slot, or way, milled in the router table.

Align the router table way marks with the sawblade. Mill the way with a series of small passes through the table saw.

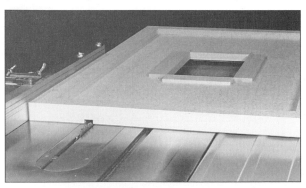

Miter gauge way/featherboard slot

PAM: There will be times when you rout the end of a board, and in that case, you need support. This is when a miter gauge comes in handy, but it needs a way (slot) to travel down. Also, you can use the way to attach featherboards, which will hold the work snug against the fence, an invaluable tool when routing thin pieces of wood. Unfortunately, you will more than likely chip the plastic laminate when you do this procedure. That just seems to be the nature of the beast.

Use your table saw and fence to mill the dado. You can use your dado blades if they are carbide tipped, otherwise, you will have to use a carbide-tipped combination blade. Don't be intimidated by the idea of using your table saw for this job. It's really the most accurate method to mill the way in the router table.

1. Remove the guide washer on the miter gauge (if you have one). Set the miter gauge on the router table. Position the miter gauge so that it doesn't get hung up on the finger guard, but you don't want the way positioned out next to the edge of the table, either. Mark the table on both sides of the miter-gauge bar. Transfer these marks over the edge of the table so you can align them with the dado blades.

2. Set the miter gauge on the table saw and adjust the blade height flush with the miter-gauge bar. You don't want slop in the way. Don't take off too much at once, and keep checking the way with the miter gauge bar.

3. Align the way marks on the router table with the sawblade. If you are using dado blades at $^3/_4$ in. width, then you will probably have to make only one pass; center the blades with the miter-gauge marks. If you are using a combination blade, start at one edge, make a pass and move the fence over a bit. Work your way over to the other mark. Quit when you get close, then check

the way with the miter gauge. Mill the way until the miter-gauge bar fits. You want the miter gauge to slide easily down the way; if it's a little tight, mill the way just a fraction wider.

The router-table switch

PAM: Install the switch and plug combination for the router. **NEVER REACH UNDER THE TABLE TO TURN ON/OFF THE ROUTER.** You might grab a handful of bit instead of the switch, and that would cause serious injury to your hand. If you have opted for a table-mount switch (like mine) instead of a floor switch, mount the switch on a router leg. I set mine on the leg, right underneath the apron so that it's out of the way, but I have easy access to it. My switch is on the outfeed side (left-hand) of the table; if I have to hang onto something, I do so with my right hand and shut off the router switch with my left. Tack the switch to either leg and play around with it (unplugged) to find out what is the best placement for you.

Attach the switch to scrap lumber, and then attach the lumber to the table.

You now have a router table, which will be the envy of all those woodworkers who don't.

One part of this switch plugs into the wall, the other part plugs into the router plug. This way the router is turned off and on by the table switch, and you don't have to stick your hand up under the table.

Router Table Safety

Always unplug your router when changing bits or working on the machine.

With the router unplugged, rotate the bit by hand to make sure it clears the router bit insert and the fence clearance. If you are using the fence, make sure it is clamped down.

Always use the finger guard. The finger guard should be positioned as close to the wood as possible, but not so close that you can't push the wood underneath it. Make sure the finger guard clears the bit.

Use pushsticks and featherboards. Hold-down wheels are a great safety feature for a router table. Be sure to clamp both ends of the fence to the table or else the wheels will lift the fence off the table.

9 BUILDING A CABINET

This four-shelf router-bit wall cabinet is made from poplar with a birch panel door. It measures 4-1/8 in. deep by 20 in. wide by 29-1/2 in. high.

PAM: This cabinet can be used to house just about anything, depending on its height and shelf depth. I use mine to store router bits, which I used to keep in cigar boxes. It's the perfect application.

As with the shop furnishings described earlier, the dimensions of this cabinet are up to you. The dimensions I used are shown on the drawing, but feel free to modify them.

Cabinet Materials

PAM: The sides, top, bottom, and shelves of this cabinet are made from ³/₄-in. hardwood; the door and back panel are ¹/₄-in. hardwood plywood. While you can certainly build your first cabinet from pine, I recommend poplar, a clear, lightweight, easy to work hardwood that finishes beautifully and is relatively inexpensive. Whatever you decide, use ³/₄-in. lumber, since ¹/₂-in. wood won't allow enough room for the rabbets and dadoes. Have the lumberyard plane the faces of the boards for you if the lumber is in the rough.

On the door panel, don't be tempted to substitute fir plywood for hardwood plywood. You can purchase hardwood plywood to match your cabinet lumber if you use birch, cherry, oak, mahogany, or walnut, to mention a few. If your cabinet lumber is poplar, a contrasting hardwood plywood is a nice choice.

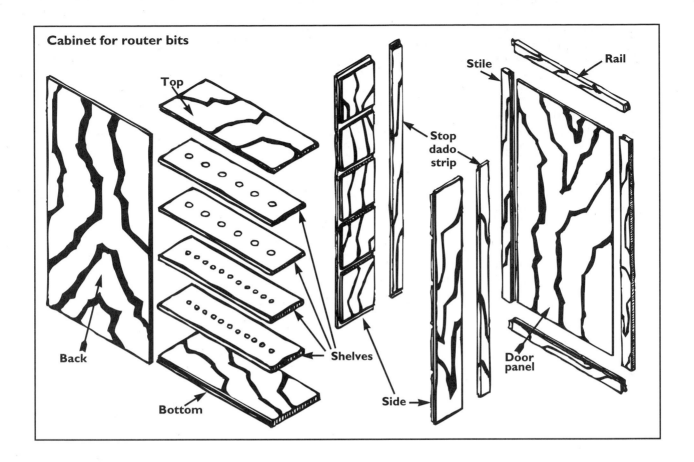

Cabinet for router bits

Top

Back

Bottom

Shelves

Stop dado strip

Side

Stile

Rail

Door panel

Dimensioning Your Cabinet

PAUL: If you don't want to use our dimensions, here's how to approach coming up with your own.

Cabinet length

PAUL: How tall do you want your cabinet? The number of shelves, and the distance between them, establishes cabinet length. And that, of course, depends on what you are going to use the cabinet for. If you construct a router-bit cabinet, then consider the tallest bit size. How many shelves do you want? (Pam used four.) Also, keep the space even between the shelves; after you have built this cabinet and understand the construction, you can start playing around with dimensions.

With a router-bit cabinet, don't drill the holes for the router-bit shanks all the way through the shelf; instead, sink holes about $1/2$-in. deep. There are two reasons for doing this: First, the shrinking and swelling of the wood with seasonal changes in humidity could trap the bits if the shanks went all the way through the shelves. Second, a straight bit would fall right through a hole drilled clear through the shelf.

Pam's tallest bit was 4 in., and to this we added 1 in. of headroom to allow removing the bit from the shelf. Therefore, we needed 5 in. between shelves. Factoring in the dadoes and rabbets (and extra at the bottom to make it easier to align and glue the shelves) we came up with a total rough length of about 33 in.; the finished cabinet length is $29^1/_2$ in.

Cabinet depth and shelf width

PAM: The width of the shelves determines the width of the sides. I used the width of my router bits as a guide and came up with a 3-in. shelf. Then I had to add in the $^1/_4$-in. back panel, and the 1-in. stop dado strip on the cabinet front. (The stop dado strip is ripped off the front edge of each side piece, then glued back on after the dadoes have been milled to hide where the dado and shelf edges meet.) The total depth of the cabinet was thus $4^1/_4$ in.

Shelf length and cabinet width

PAM: I wanted a 20-in. overall cabinet width. Since all the dadoes and rabbets are $^3/_8$ in. deep (half the thickness of $^3/_4$-in. lumber), the shelf length had to be $19^1/_4$ inches.

Cabinet top and bottom pieces

PAM: The top and bottom pieces are the same length as the shelves, but must be the same width as the sides—$4^1/_4$ in.

Door and back panels

PAM: Roughly estimate both the front and back panels as the same width and length as the finished cabinet. In this case, you'll need two pieces of $^1/_4$-in. hardwood plywood measuring 20 in. wide by $29^1/_2$ in. long.

Stiles and rails

PAM: The stiles are the vertical pieces on each side of the door, the rails are the horizontal pieces; both stiles and rails are grooved to accept the door. The stiles and rails can be as wide as you want—depending on the size of the cabinet. If it's a small cabinet, they won't be very wide. The stiles and rails on my cabinet were $1^3/_4$ in. wide, but rails can be wider than the stiles if you think it will improve the appearance.

Bill of Materials, Hardware, and Tools

PAUL: You can run out and buy as much hardwood as you think you might need, or you can roughly figure the board footage first. I usually have wood on hand, because when I see boards that are exceptionally beautiful or unusual, I buy them. But even though I've got a stack of lumber to choose from when I build something, I always seem to come up short—and the middle of a project is not the time to find out this one little detail. Draft a bill of materials first, and then you'll know the minimum amount of wood you will need to buy. I always have a column for rough dimensions to allow for jointing, saw kerfs, and minor mistakes.

Refer to Chapter 5 to figure the board footage needed, then add 10 percent for waste.

This is how the bill of material looks.

Piece	No.	Thickness	Rough width	Finish width	Rough length	Finish length
Top	1	3/4"	5"	4 1/4"	20"	19 1/4"
Bottom	1	3/4"	5"	4 1/4"	20"	19 1/4"
Sides	2	3/4"	5"	4 1/4"	33"	29 1/2"
Shelves	4	3/4"	4"	3"	20"	19 1/4"
Stiles	2	3/4"	2"	1 3/4"	30"	29 1/2"
Rails	2	3/4"	2"	1 3/4"	20"	19 1/4"
Door panel	1	1/4"	20"	*	29 1/2"	*
Back panel	1	1/4"	20"	19 1/4"	30"	29 1/2"

* Because the door panel will be cut to fit the grooves in the edges of the stiles and rails by transfer of measurement, you can't know the finish dimensions yet.

We built Pam's cabinet out of three ³/₄-in. by 5-in. by 96-in. boards.

Tools and hardware:

- Cabinet hinges (2)
- Doorknob
- Door catch
- Spiral bit, 2-in. cutting length with down spiral (a down spiral moves the chips away from the router)
- Featherboards
- Slot-cutter, ⁵/₃₂-in., 3-wing. This will be used to cut the grooves in the stiles and rails for the door panel.
- Chisels
- Hold-down wheels for your router table (optional, but really nice)

Lumber Preparation

PAM: The lumber has to be milled square for the cabinet to fit together. No sense trying to square lumber if your saw blade and miter gauge aren't true.

1. With your try-square, check that the saw-blade is at 90 degrees to the table. Adjust accordingly.

2. Square the miter gauge against the table, or check it for square, with your try-square against the blade.

To make a square cabinet, you have to square all the boards. You still have to joint one edge so the bow is taken out of the board. You then use this one straight edge to square up the rest of the board.

I rough-cut my lumber into shorter lengths—the shorter the board, the less bow, and the less wood to be jointed off. Once the edge is jointed straight, I place the straight edge against the table-saw fence, and adjust the fence to rip off just enough wood to take the bow out of the opposite edge.

Set the outfeed fence flush with the spiral router bit using a straight piece of wood.

Setting up for router-table jointing

PAM: Make sure the fender washers are in place between the wood and the polypropylene so your fence will behave like a jointer fence.

1. Adjust the height of the spiral bit to just a little above the edge of the board.

2. To adjust the fence for jointing, place a straight piece of wood against the outfeed fence and over the bit clearance. Move the fence over until the wood is just touching the spiral bit. Clamp the fence in place.

3. Set the finge rguard to a fraction above the surface of the lumber you are going to joint. A finger guard won't do you any good if it's too high.

Jointing the wood

PAM: Don't just turn on the router and go. You first have to determine the bowed edge. Set the board on the router-table top or the table-saw top—the edge that has the center that clears the table, even if only by a fraction, is the edge you want to joint. If you joint the other edge, the wood will follow the curve and jointing won't accomplish anything.

Once you have determined the bow, you have to figure out which way the grain is running, because you want to joint with the grain, not against it. Looking down over the top of the fence and bit, the bit turns counter-clockwise— you want to feed the wood right to left.

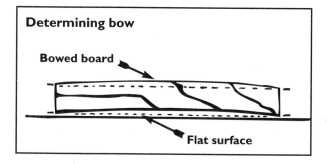

Whenever possible, the wood grain should slope away from the router cutter, otherwise the grain will tear out.

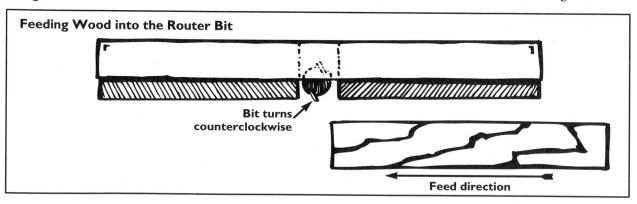

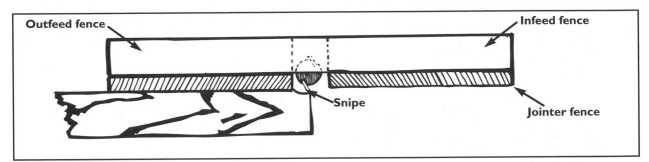

The cutter will snipe the end of the board, unless the outfeed fence is offset to the depth of the cut.

Jointing usually requires at least several passes through the bit. Hold the board firmly against the fence as it enters the cutter. Pay particular attention to the lumber when the board is about 6 to 8 in. past the cutter—this part of the board has to stay against the fence. While pushing the board through the cutter, apply side pressure against the outfeed fence, to keep the board from wandering.

Make a pass at the edge of the board and then examine the edge. If you haven't removed any wood, the fence and bit aren't aligned, that is, the fence is too far in front of the cutter. Realign the fence, and make another pass at the board. If you still aren't taking off any wood, and you are sure the bit is aligned with the fence, then check the bow of the board — you might be working on the wrong surface. Or your fence might be warped.

If the outfeed fence isn't set flush with the cutter, extra wood will be removed at the very end of the cut, creating a dip called snipe. This is a clue to readjust the fence. Then joint each board until it has a smooth, straight edge.

Making the Cabinet Parts

PAUL: The cabinet sides require the most work, since they are both rabbeted and dadoed. The top and bottom pieces of the cabinet are rabbeted. To avoid changing blades and adjusting them to height a million times (all rabbets and dadoes are ³/₈ in. deep), mill the sides, top, and bottom together.

1. Crosscut both sides to rough length (oversize by 2 to 3 in.)

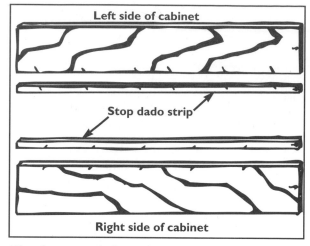

Rip the stop dado strips off the cabinet sides. Diagonal pencil marks keep the strips from being swapped. Arrows show cabinet top.

The recess cut into the auxiliary dado fence lets you vary the width of a rabbet cut without restacking a thinner dado set.

2. Crosscut the top and bottom pieces to rough length. Label all pieces if you haven't already done so.

3. Rip the cabinet sides to finished width. Don't cut the top and bottom pieces to width yet—you'll rip them to width later, along with the shelves.

Marking the cabinet sides and cutting the stop dado strips

1. Orient the sides the way you want them in the final cabinet. Mark the sides as shown in the drawing.

2. Rip off the stop dado strips from both cabinet sides.

3. Before you change blades, cut your locating pin. This strip of wood measures 2 in. long, $^3/_4$ in. wide, and a fraction less than $^3/_8$ in. thick—you'll use it later to help evenly space the shelf dadoes.

Cutting the rabbets

PAM: You should already have an auxiliary dado fence from making the workbench in the previous chapter. If you cut it up for something else, then make a new one. If you haven't already dadoed a fence clearance, do so now. All rabbets and dadoes required for the shelves, top, and bottom pieces are $^3/_4$ in. wide; the rabbets for the back panel are equal to the thickness of the plywood (about $^1/_4$ in.). The point is, you will be using only a part of the dado blade, and you need to cut a recess in the auxiliary fence so you can adjust the fence over the blades; this eliminates having to restack the blades to different widths.

1. Stack the dado blades $^3/_4$ in. wide. Retract the blades below the surface of the table.

2. Attach the auxiliary dado fence to the table-saw fence.

3. Lay a scrap of ³/₄-in. particleboard flat on the table and against the auxiliary dado fence. Mark the thickness of the particleboard on the fence.

4. Move the fence over so that at least half of the auxiliary fence is directly over the dado blades. Lock the fence. If you can't see any blades, the fence is too far over and the blades will chew the heck out of the metal fence.

5. Turn on the saw, and slowly raise the dado blade until it reaches the mark on the fence. Shut off the saw.

6. The cabinet sides, plus the stop dado strips, are rabbeted at the top edge to accept the cabinet top. Set the dado blade height to half the thickness of the lumber. You are going to run scrap until you get it right.

7. Place the auxiliary dado fence right at the very edge of the dado blades—you want the full ³/₄ in. width but no more. This gets touchy, since you've cut away part of the auxiliary dado fence and can't use it for an accurate rabbet reading. But you're going to check, using scrap, to see if you've got it right. Use a couple of pieces of scrap that are comfortably long. Don't use short stuff you can't hang onto.

8. Using the miter gauge to brace the wood, rabbet the end of a piece of scrap.

9. Determine if the fence is set at the correct distance. Place the rabbet against the edge of a piece of wood intended for use in the cabinet; the end of the rabbet should be flush with the edge of the board. If not, adjust the fence accordingly.

10. To set the blade for exactly half the thickness of the board, cut a rabbet on the edge of a piece of scrap that is the same thickness as the boards being used for the cabinet.

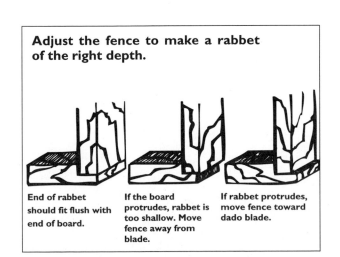

Adjust the fence to make a rabbet of the right depth.

End of rabbet should fit flush with end of board.

If the board protrudes, rabbet is too shallow. Move fence away from blade.

If rabbet protrudes, move fence toward dado blade.

After cutting the first dado kerf, move the miter-gauge extension 5 in. from the outside edge of that kerf. The extension is then secured to the miter gauge, and a second dado kerf is cut.

Set the locating pin in the dado. If the pin is a little loose, glue it in place.

Cut the scrap in half and put the rabbeted edges together—the top surface should be flush. If they are not, adjust the blade.

11. Rabbet the top of each cabinet side piece.

12. Rabbet the top of each stop dado strip.

Cutting the dadoes

The dadoes are milled using the miter-gauge extension (shown in Chapter 6) to which has been attached a $3/8$-in. by $3/4$-in. locating pin to ensure evenly spaced shelf dadoes. Here's how it works: After the first dado is cut, it is placed over the locating pin and the next shelf dado is cut; then that dado is placed over the locating pin, and so on until all the dadoes are cut.

Remove the table-saw fence, but don't take off the auxiliary dado fence. You'll need it again when you are done with the shelf dadoes.

1. Attach a miter-gauge extension about the length of the sides to the miter gauge.

2. Dado the miter-gauge extension to create a kerf reference.

3. To figure the shelf-space distance, you will probably have to use a tape measure. Remove the miter-gauge extension. Starting at the outside edge of the kerf cut on the extension, mark to the left for the shelf-space distance. My shelf space was 5 in., so I measured 5 in. to the left and marked the fence.

4. Align the mark with the outside edge of the dado blade. Reattach the fence and make another kerf cut.

5. Check to make sure you have the shelf-spacedistance between the dadoes correct. If not, move the fence to an area that hasn't been cut and repeat the two previous steps.

6. Place the locating pin in the first dado kerf you milled.

Dadoing the sides for the shelves

1. Place the top rabbet over the locating pin.

2. Mill the dado in the side.

3. Place the dado you just milled on top of the locating pin. Mill another dado. Clean off the shavings after each pass—you want everything riding on the table, not on top of the shavings (your dadoes will become shallower as the shavings build up). Continue until you are ready to mill the last dado.

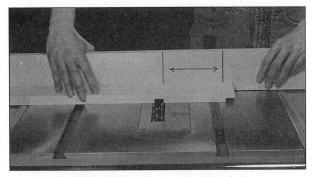

Place the rabbet on the top of the cabinet side over the locating pin.

The stop dado strip

PAM: The stop dado strip and the last shelf dado are milled together. You have to align the stop dado strip with its respective side so that the top dado can be cut in both pieces at the same time.

Here the top dado, the four dadoes for the shelves, and the bottom dado have all been cut.

1. Place the next-to-last dado on the locating pin. Place the corresponding stop dado strip at the leading edge of the side. Make sure the top ends of the side and stop dado strip are flush and match.

2. Hold the side and stop dado firmly together and mill the remaining bottom dado.

3. Repeat for the remaining cabinet side and stop dado strip.

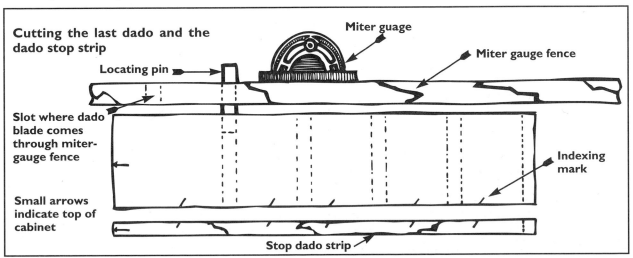

Cutting the last dado and the dado stop strip

Miter guage

Miter gauge fence

Locating pin

Slot where dado blade comes through miter-gauge fence

Indexing mark

Small arrows indicate top of cabinet

Stop dado strip

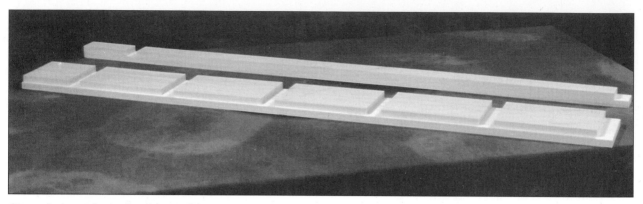

Stop dado strip and cabinet side.

Cutting the remaining rabbets

PAM: Match each cabinet side with its corresponding stop dado strip. Mark the back edge of each side for the rabbet that will accept the cabinet back.

The top and bottom pieces are also rabbeted to accept the back panel—mark them. Don't change the blade height—it remains half the thickness of the ³/₄-in. lumber.

Put the auxiliary dado fence back on the table saw. The rabbet width is the thickness of the ¹/₄-in. plywood used for the back, which is probably not a full ¹/₄ in. thick. Use the plywood to transfer the rabbet width.

1. Set the plywood on edge, over or in front of the dado blades. The plywood should align with the outside edge of the dado blades. Move the fence over against the plywood. Lock the fence.

Use a cabinet side to adjust the table saw to cut the shelves to width. Lock the fence, remove the side, and mill the shelves.

2. Test for rabbet width. Rabbet a piece of scrap. Check the rabbet with the plywood thickness—the surfaces should be flush. If they aren't, adjust the fence accordingly.

3. Rabbet the top piece the length of the edge you marked. Do the same with the bottom piece.

4. Rabbet each cabinet side down the length of the back edge. When you do this, all the dadoes face the table. If the dadoes are facing up, you've got the wrong side, or the wrong piece, or both.

Constructing the shelves

PAM: Change blades, because now you're back to ripping and crosscutting.

1. Lower the sawblade to fit underneath the rabbet.

2. Place the cabinet side between the fence and the blade. Push the side over until the blade is underneath the rabbet. Lock the fence.

3. Remove the side piece. Raise the blade to ¹/₄ in. higher than the shelf thickness.

4. Rip each shelf piece to width.

5. To mill the shelf, top, and bottom pieces to length, locate the square end on each piece; this is the end that fits against the

stop block. Otherwise, you might cut all of the pieces out of square. The shelves, top, and bottom are all the same length.

6. Crosscut the first piece to length.

7. Set up the miter-gauge extension and use a stop block for the remaining pieces. Crosscut the remaining shelves, top, and bottom to length. Set the top and bottom aside.

Jointing the front sides and the stop dado strip

PAM: To ensure a tight, straight, even joint between the stop dado strip and the side, you need to joint both the edge of the cabinet side and the edge of the stop dado strip.

1. Put the jointing fence on the router table.

   Set the spiral bit in the router and adjust the height of the bit 1/8 in. above the wood.

2. Joint the edge of the first cabinet side.

3. Joint the edge of the second cabinet side.

   When you get to the narrow stop dado strips, use your featherboard. Place it at the outfeed side of the bit, not at the bit clearance or the infeed side of the bit. On a jointing cut, the board needs to be held against the outfeed fence. Also, you want the featherboard snug against the wood, but not so tight that you can't push the board through easily; if the featherboard is too loose, you might as well not even use it—which is a bad idea. It usually takes a few trial runs to get the featherboard positioned correctly.

1. Clamp the featherboard in place against the outfeed jointer fence.

2. On your first stop dado strip, joint the edge that will mate with the jointed edge of the cabinet side. Push the stop dado

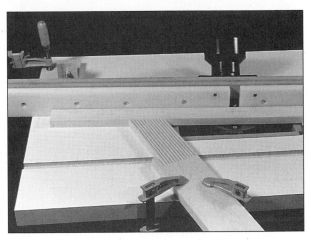

Hold the stop dado strip against the outfeed fence of the router table with a securely clamped featherboard.

strip clear of the bit with a piece of scrap. Once the strip is clear, hang onto the scrap, and shut off the router.

3. Joint the other stop dado strip.

Completing the cabinet sides

PAM: Everything straight? Good. Time to get gluing. Have ready a scrap strip of 3/4-in. particleboard to align the bottom dado of the side and stop dado strips during gluing.

1. Spread glue on the cabinet side, not on the stop dado strip—you'll have more control over the glue when you work on the side. (You want to keep glue out of the dadoes, so you don't have to chisel it out later.)

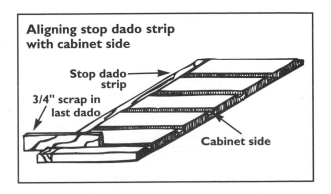

Aligning stop dado strip with cabinet side

Stop dado strip

3/4" scrap in last dado

Cabinet side

2. Slide the cabinet side and stop dado strip together. Align the pieces with the scrap strip.

3. Clamp the pieces together. Remove the scrap strip after the clamps have been tightened—you don't want it glued into the dado.

4. Repeat these steps for the second cabinet side and stop dado.

5. Scrape off any dried excess glue. If you have glue in the dadoes, carefully chisel it out or the shelves won't fit.

Drilling the router-bit holes in the shelf

PAM: If the cabinet is being used to house router bits, then lay out the holes for them. I dedicated three of my shelves to $1/2$-in. shank bits and one shelf to $1/4$-in. shank bits, but you can arrange your storage however you please.

1. Place the jointed edge of the shelf so it faces the front of the cabinet after the holes are drilled.

2. Mark the shelves for bit-shank placement. You can divide the space any way you want.

3. The shelves are $3/4$ in. thick, but you don't want the holes any deeper than $1/2$ in. Use a depth collar on the bit or a masking tape flag to indicate correct depth. To drill the holes for the $1/2$-in. shank bits, I used a

$33/64$-in. bit ($1/64$ in larger than $1/2$ in.); likewise, for $1/4$-in. shank bits, use a $17/64$-in. bit. Set the bit at the edge of the board and mark the bit for depth.

4. Clamp the shelf down, and drill the holes.

Trimming the bottom cabinet sides

PAM: You are going to cut the outside shoulder off the bottom dado, thus turning it into a rabbet to accept the cabinet bottom. You have to be careful here: If you make the cut too deep into the dado, the rabbet will be too shallow and the bottom piece won't fit flush with the ends of the sides.

1. Use a miter extension with a stop block. Align the bottom edge of the dado with the sawblade. You want to remove the wood starting at the shoulder of the dado.

2. Crosscut the excess wood from both cabinet sides.

Trimming the top and bottom to width

1. Transfer the width: Set a cabinet side between the fence and blade. Lock the fence. If you want, shave a little of the front edge off each side. This will true the sides if there is any deviation, and also ensure that the top and bottom widths, when ripped, will be the same as the sides.

2. Rip the top piece to width.

3. Rip the bottom piece to width.

4. Joint the front edges on the sides, top, and bottom.

Trimming the back to width and length

1. Transfer the length of a shelf: Place a shelf lengthwise between the blade and the fence. Lock the fence and remove the shelf piece.

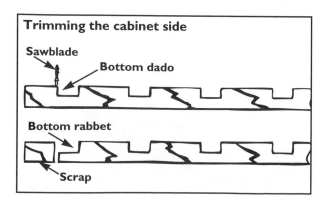

Trimming the cabinet side

Sawblade

Bottom dado

Bottom rabbet

Scrap

2. When milling a piece of ¼-in. plywood, raise the blade a bit higher than you normally would—but don't get radical about it. Accidents happen when the blade is only ⅛ in. above the wood and the plywood crawls up on top of the blade.

3. Rip the back piece to width.

4. Dry-fit and clamp the cabinet sides, top, and bottom together. If the shelves are a real bear to get in and out of the dadoes, you can leave them out for this.

5. Fit the back panel between the sides and in the top rabbet. Mark the back panel to length, where it meets the inside of the bottom rabbet. It's better to go a little long on this and then nibble it down to a tight fit than to cut it too short. The back is what keeps the cabinet square.

6. Crosscut the back panel to length.

7. Loosen the clamps, and reclamp with the back panel in place.

Constructing The Door

PAM: The door panel floats in a groove cut in each rail and stile. The grooves are cut using the slot cutter and a router table. The rails join to the stiles by a tongue, which you cut on the table saw.

Milling the stiles and rails

PAM: The stiles and rails of this cabinet are both the same width. When sizing stiles and rails, try to keep them in scale with the size of the door: Very wide stiles and rails on a small cabinet might look ridiculous; likewise, thin stiles and rails might be dwarfed by a big cabinet. For my cabinet I used a stile and rail width of 1¾ in. Rip all the stile and rail pieces to width, then crosscut both stiles to length.

Raise the sawblade higher than normal when cutting thin plywood, to prevent it from creeping on top of the blade and kicking back.

You want smooth edges on the stiles and rails, because any variation will jump right out at you and look sloppy. And since you're at it, joint the outside edges, too. This way, it won't matter which edge you put the groove in.

Milling the grooves

PAM: Since the plywood door panel fits inside the grooves, the width of the groove is the thickness of the panel. To mill the groove, use the slot cutter in a router table. You will have to use a bearing with the slot cutter since it is designed that way; use the smallest bearing so it's not in the way.

1. Place the slot cutter in the router; place the router fence on the table. Does the slot cutter clear the fence? If not, mark on either side of the slot cutter, and also mark for the height.

Enlarge the router-bit clearance hole in the fence by crosscutting on the table saw with a combination blade.

Raise the slot-cutter bit close to the center of the door stile. Pass the stile through the cutter and then flip it end for end; pass the stile through the cutter again.

2. Using a miter-gauge extension, crosscut the bit clearance to the marks. Now you're ready to position the ½-in. deep groove in the edge; use the same thickness of scrap lumber to locate the groove close to the middle. If you use a piece of scrap that isn't the same thickness as the wood for the stiles and rails, the groove won't be accurate.

3. Place the wood on top of the slot cutter, right next to the bearing. Pull the fence over until it's flush with the edge of the wood. Look down over the top of the fence—you can see the edge of the wood, bearing, and fence all line up.

Mill the rail tongue on the table saw. The joint should slip together snugly.

Think back, remember when you centered the dado on the stretcher; you eyeballed it, ran a dado at about the center, and then turned the board end-for-end and made another dado, and presto, the dado was centered? Use that technique to center the groove and also set the groove width. The trick to centering this way is to always make two passes: You make the first pass, then you turn the board end-for-end and make the second pass. Use scrap large enough to handle comfortably.

4. Set the edge of the wood against the slot cutter. Adjust the bit depth to what you think is about the center.

5. Mill the groove. Turn the board end-for-end, with the same edge against the fence. Make another pass through the bit. You should be removing very little wood.

6. Check the groove with the plywood edge. Does it fit?

7. If the groove is too tight, lower the bit a hair. Again, make two passes through the bit. If you don't, the groove will be offset and then you have to mill all the tongues off-center, and that's something we are not going to embark on.

8. If the groove is loose, raise the bit a hair. Use another piece of scrap and mill the groove again. Remember, make two passes, end-for-end. Continue until you have the correct groove width. The plywood should fit snugly in the groove.

9. Mill a groove on the inside edge of each stile. Do the same with the rails.

10. Mill a spare rail to use for setting the dimension of the rail tongue. Clamp the stiles into place at the edges of the cabinet.

Milling the rail tongues

PAM: The rail tongue fits inside the groove on the stile. Use your table saw to mill this piece; it's a rabbet-type cut, and you will use your fence to set dimensions. Use the spare rail for setting tongue dimensions. Clearances here are very tight. Before you cut the tongues, you have to cut the rails to length.

1. Clamp a rail at the inside edge of the stile groove. At the other end, mark the rail where it meets the inside edge of the opposite stile groove.

2. Crosscut each rail to marked length.

3. To set tongue dimensions, place the spare rail against the inside edge of the stile groove. Mark the goove depth on the spare rail at the outside edge of the stile.

4. Before you set the fence, you have to set the blade height for the tongue. Place the spare rail next to the blade. Raise the blade until it's right at the bottom edge of the groove.

5. Set the fence. Place the mark for the outside of the stile at the outside of the blade. Don't set the fence for the entire tongue length. It's better to nibble away than cut the tongue too long.

6. With the spare rail, start at the end and work your way toward the fence. Support the wood with your miter gauge.

7. Mill the tongue on one side, turn the piece over, and mill the other side. Make a few passes at the tongue before you check for fit. You need to mill enough tongue to fit into the groove so you can get an accurate reading; no more than a quarter inch of tongue will do.

8. Place the tongue in the groove. How does if fit? Too tight, raise the sawblade; too

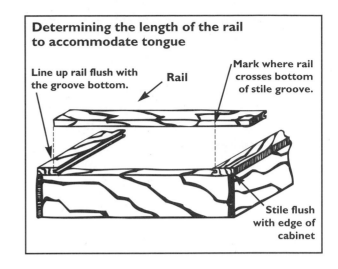

Determining the length of the rail to accommodate tongue

Line up rail flush with the groove bottom.

Rail

Mark where rail crosses bottom of stile groove.

Stile flush with edge of cabinet

To cut a tongue that will fit its groove snugly, set the sawblade height exactly at the edge of the groove.

Cut a tongue in the spare rail, test-fit, and adjust the sawblade accordingly.

loose, lower the blade. Use the other end of the spare rail piece if you need to.

9. Rabbet the spare rail until it reaches the fence, which should be a smidgen short of the tongue length. Stop and check the tongue for fit. Place the tongue into the stile and look at the groove. You want the tongue to fit right against the inside edge of the groove. If you mill the tongue too long, the rail won't fit snugly against the stile; if this is the case, mill the other end until you get the dimension right. If the tongue is too short, it leaves a hole where it would have met the bottom of the stile groove; try to avoid this if possible.

10. When you have set the dimension for a perfect tongue, mill the tongues in each end of the rails.

11. Dry-fit the rails in place. Clamp the stile and rail assembly in position on the front of the cabinet. This is starting to look good, isn't it?

Constructing the door panel

PAM: The door panel fits inside the grooves on all edges.

Here the stiles, rails, and door panel are ready for sanding and assembly.

1. To rip the plywood to width, unclamp and remove one of the rails. The width of the door panel is equal to the length of the rail including the tongues. Transfer the width: Place the rail lengthwise between the blade and the fence. Lock the fence.

2. Rip the plywood to width.

3. Next, crosscut the plywood to length. The height of the door panel is equal to the length of the stile, less the width of both the top and bottom rail tongues. To transfer the measurement to the plywood, unclamp the other rail. Transfer the length of the stile to the edge of the plywood.

4. Put the two outside edges of the rails together. The tongues shouldn't have any gaps between them. Lay the tongues on the plywood just below the stile length mark. Draw a line on the other side of the tongues.

5. Crosscut the panel to length.

6. Slide all the door pieces together.

SANDING

PAM: Before you glue the cabinet together, you need to sand the pieces that end up inside the cabinet, otherwise, you won't be able to get at them. You don't have to sand the outside of the cabinet until after you've glued it up.

1. Sand the shelves and the interior face of the top and bottom pieces; stay away from all the edges. Don't sand rabbets or dadoes, because you'll change their size.

2. Sand the interior face of the back panel.

3. Sand the front and back of the door panel. Once the stiles and rails are glued together, it's difficult to sand the panel's corners.

Assembling the Cabinet

PAM: The whole piece goes together at once, so have plenty of clamps on hand; use polyurethane glue. Read the instructions through once before you begin. Once you get started, you have to stay with it.

Before you begin, make a squaring stick, like the one shown in the drawing, to check the cabinet for square once you get a few clamps on.

The gluing sequence

PAM: Remember, know what you're doing before you begin, since you can't stop once you start.

1. Glue the shelves. Spread the glue on the sides and bottom of each dado. Position the shelf in the dado. Continue until all shelves are in position.

2. Glue the top and bottom pieces. Spread glue on the rabbets and position the top piece, with the rabbet at the back of the cabinet. Clamp across the width. Repeat with the bottom piece.

3. Place the cabinet so the back is facing up; you should be looking at the rabbet on all four edges.

4. Glue the back panel. Run a bead of glue around the rabbet. Don't get carried away here—the squeezeout will end up inside the cabinet. Set the back panel in place, and clamp the top and bottom edge to hold the panel in place.

5. Turn the cabinet over so the front is facing up. Place clamps on the front edge reaching to the back panel to pull it in tight and secure the back panel in the rabbet.

6. To check for square, set the point of the squaring stick in a corner of the cabinet.

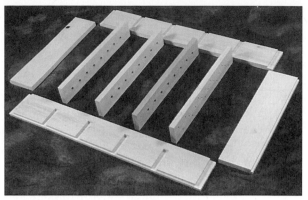

Before beginning glue-up, lay out the parts in correct relationship to each other.

Clamps apply pressure to all joints while the glue sets.

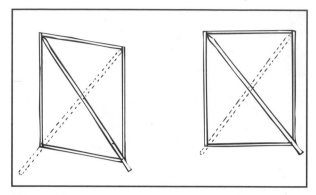

The cabinet is square when both diagonals are the same length.

Pencil a mark on the stick where it meets the opposite corner.

7. Measure the opposite diagonal. If the marks don't meet, the cabinet is out of square. If they do meet, your cabinet is square; continue clamping, placing a clamp wherever you see a gap. If your cabinet isn't square, then you have to "rack" it into square. This means you shorten one diagonal while lengthening the other.

8. Loosen the clamps across the ends of the cabinet. Place a pipe clamp diagonally across the corners that give the longest measurement. Gently tighten the clamp. Check both diagonal measurements. Are they equal? If not, keep gently tightening the clamp until they are.

Lay the hinge in position on the cabinet edge. Draw a line around the hinge leaf.

Gluing the door

PAM: The panel in the door floats. Don't glue it in.

1. If the door is together, remove the rails. Spread glue on the tongues and reassemble the door.

2. Place a clamp across each rail and tighten the stiles to the rails.

More sanding

PAUL: Do your sanding now, before you set the hinges. If you wait until afterward, you could inadvertently deform the level surface.

1. Sand the entire outside of the cabinet.

2. Sand the stiles and rails.

Installing the hinges

PAM: Since I don't know what you are using for a doorknob and catch, you're on your own. But I will tell you how to mount the hinges. Get out your chisels. The hinge plates are recessed into the wood so they are flush with the edge surface. If they aren't, the door won't close. Try this on scrap first, to get the hang of using a chisel.

Place the hinge on the cabinet first, and then transfer the placement to the door.

1. Figure out on which side you want the door to open. (The door should hinge on the left for right-handed users, and vice-versa for left-handed users.) Mark the corresponding edge for the hinges. The hinges are placed close to the top, but not at the top, otherwise the door will warp. Go look at any door in your house for reference. Use your combination square and mark a few inches down from the top and the same distance up from the bottom. These marks will locate the outside limits of the hinge plate.

2. Place the hinge on the edge of the board at the mark. At this point the hinge can be opened or closed, it doesn't matter. The hinge pin side rests at the outside edge of the cabinet. Draw a line around the hinge with a pencil.

3. Remove the hinge. Use a utility knife to score the three edges right inside the pencil line; if you score on the line, or even outside the line, the hinge recess will be too big.

4. Pencil parallel lines from the scored edge to the outside cabinet edge. Keep the lines close together.

5. If you have one, use a chisel with a blade the width of the hinge recess. Place the chisel on the parallel pencil mark and give it a good rap. Ultimately, you want the chisel to score the depth of the hinge plate thickness—which isn't much. Score all parallel lines with the chisel.

6. Set the chisel at the end of the scored hinge recess and chisel across the score marks. You are chiseling lengthwise across the recess and the grain. The pieces of wood should pop right out.

7. Check the fit of the hinge plate. The hinge has to fit flush with the surface of the edge. Chisel out more of the recess if needed. Take your time—be careful not to chisel too deeply, because this can't be corrected and can be seen at quite a distance.

8. Position the door on the cabinet and transfer the hinge plate location to the door stile.

9. Repeat these steps for the remaining hinge-plate recesses.

10. Fit the hinges into the recesses, and mark the holes for the screws. Pilot-drill before fastening. Attach the hinges.

Score the wood with a chisel to a depth equal to the hinge thickness. This will allow you to chisel out the waste without chipping the wood.

Finishing

PAM: You should be proud of this cabinet, so put a nice finish on it. If you have used an open-grained wood, like oak, I suggest you experiment with shellac; this is what I use on my open-grain woods. Shellac gives a shiny finish and it's fast to apply—I love it.

Wiping varnish is another option. This will take much longer than shellac to apply, and gives a completely different look and feel. I make my own from three parts mineral spirits to one part varnish, and though you can wipe it on with a lint-free cloth, I usually brush it on. Give the piece two or three coats.

Remove all hardware prior to applying the finish; replace the hardware after the finish material has dried thoroughly. You're now ready to hang the cabinet on the wall, and start purchasing router bits to fill it up.

SUPPLIERS

Woodworker's Supply, Inc.
5604 A1ameda Place, NE
Albuquerque, NM 87113-2100
1-800-645-9292
 Machinery, power tools, dust collection systems, shop accessories, polypropylene (UHMW), clamps, finishing supplies, etc.

Eagle America
P.O. Box 1099
Chardon, Ohio 44024
1-800-872-2511
 Router bits, saw blades, router table top and router table accessories

Grizzly Imports, Inc.
West of the Mississippi:
 P.O. Box 2069
 Bellingham, WA 98227
 1-800-541-5537

East of the Mississippi:
 2406 Reach Road
 Williamsport, PA 17701
 1-800-523-4777
 Machinery, power tools, dust collection systems, shop accessories.

Trend Lines, Inc.
Woodworking Supplies
135 American Legion Highway
P.O. Box 9117
Revere, MA 02151-9117
l-800-767-9999
 Machinery, power tools, clamps, shop accessories.

Klingspor's Sanding Catalog
P.O. Box 3737
Hickory, NC 28603-3737
 Abrasives, power tools, dust collection systems

Garrett Wade
161 Avenue of the Americas
New York, NY 10013-1299
1-800-221-2942
 Fine hand tools, chisels, tools of measurement, hand saws

Woodhaven
5323 W. Kimberly Road
Davenport, Iowa 52806-7126
1-800-344-6657
 Router table tops and accessories, router bits

Penn State Industries
2850 Comly Road
Philadelphia, PA 19154
1-800-377-7297
 Dust collection systems

MLCS Ltd
P.O. Box 4053
Rydal, PA 19046
1-800-533-9298
 Router bits

CMT Tools
310 Mears Blvd.
P.O. Box 1518
Oldsmar, FL 34677
1-800-531-5559
 Router bits, saw blades

Hartville Tool
940 West Maple St.
Hartville, Ohio 44632
1-800-345-2396
 Router table top, shop accessories, clamps

INDEX

Editor: Laura Tringali

Design and layout: Anita Pandolfi

Illustration origination: Victoria P. Jones

Scanner operator: Morgan B. Kelsey

Index: Jennifer Kelsey

General-purpose clerk: Larry Green

Printed and bound by:
Quebecor, Hawkins, TN, U.S.A.

Typeface: Adobe Garamond